STAYIN'
De-Stress your Life

By the same author

Auras and Colours:
A Guide to Working with Subtle Energies

How to Heal and Be Healed:
A Guide to Health in Times of Change

STAYING COOL
De-Stress your Life

Paul Lambillion

Newleaf

Newleaf
an imprint of
Gill & Macmillan Ltd
Hume Avenue, Park West, Dublin 12
with associated companies throughout the world
www.gillmacmillan.ie

© Paul Lambillion 2003

0 7171 3598 5

Illustrations by Vanessa Soodeen, except page 56 which is by Alanna Corballis. Based on original ideas by the author.
Design by Design Image
Print origination by Type IT, Dublin
Printed by ColourBooks Ltd, Dublin

This book is typeset in 10/15.5 Stone Informal.

The paper used in this book comes from the wood pulp of managed forests. For every tree felled, at least one tree is planted, thereby renewing natural resources.

All rights reserved.
No part of this publication may be copied, reproduced or transmitted in any form or by any means, without permission of the publishers.

A CIP catalogue record for this book is available from the British Library.

1 3 5 4 2

Contents

Introduction	ix
1. Making Space – Taking Charge	1
2. Stress and Relaxation	25
3. Exams, Tests and Interviews	54
4. Your Imagination	87
5. Happy and Positive	116
6. Problems, Feelings and Making Things Work	139
7. And so … Getting Physical!	162
Conclusion	172

This book is dedicated to young people who are the future of our world, and to those – young at heart – who see the need to improve on what has gone before.

I would like to thank those who have supported my work and the production of this book, especially the students and teachers I have worked with over the years who explored these techniques with me; also my long-suffering editor, Eveleen Coyle, who encouraged me with a mixture of wise suggestions and patient, sensitive insight.

Thank you.

Introduction

As with any book, the author always writes from his or her own needs and experience, whatever the nature of the work and the subjects it may explore. Of course, there may be elements of research, sometimes considerable, but there is invariably some process or set of ideas that have been present in the writer's mind for a time and prompted the putting of pen to paper, or fingers on the keyboard as the case may be.

This book is written firstly because I am the father of three children (I should say young people) of whom I am immensely proud – at the time of writing their ages are 26, 20 and 17. They are not perfect and they have all had their problems. Like most families we have had our desperate moments along with great joys and I won't embarrass them by listing them all here. But we have usually overcome problems together and we have always explored the ways and means of putting things right, of healing the hurts and seeking ways of avoiding or limiting unnecessary stresses and strains in the future.

Of course, we cannot avoid problems altogether. There would be no sense in that and most of us can accept, usually with hindsight, that in the overcoming of our difficulties we can develop a stronger and more effective nature. We learn how to deal with things, however much we dislike them. We discover that some things we cannot change, at least not straight away, so we learn how to work through them. And often we find that they are not as bad as we thought they would be.

The second reason for writing this book comes from my personal experience of school and examinations. I was terrified of examinations, enduring that awful sensation in the pit of the stomach that so many school boys and girls, students, and indeed adults suffer, upon entering the examination room before enduring public exams on which so much seemed to depend. Fail and you were like a leper. Pass, and enjoy success, but then you simply prepared for the next pile of tests and assessments.

However, in my school and college days, such experiences didn't come around with the rapidity and intensity that they do today. It is generally accepted that, in the UK at least, our school pupils are probably the most tested and assessed in Europe.

The social pressures are also greater on young people today. We live in an extremely material world where everything is driven by image and appearance, and fame and fortune are seen as the only worthwhile aspirations for young people. A senior teacher in one comprehensive school I visited recently to teach unstressing skills to 17-year olds was most concerned that we do not always give young people satisfactory strategies to cope with these pressures nor is there any longer a significant moral or spiritual underpinning to provide the sound platform needed to make the choices young people have to face. As a relatively

Introduction

senior member of that society, I apologise to the young people reading the book, and hope this text goes some way to rectifying things a little.

We consider choice to be freedom, but our ever-expanding choice simply tends to bring more stress and pressure. We are bombarded with choice and, presumably, spend more money on yet more acquisitions. A deputy head teacher who is also a client of mine told me that during the summer of 2001, seven 15–16 year olds were admitted to a local hospital, no longer able to cope with the demands being made upon them both in the lead up to and during examination time. The teacher is a conscientious, very experienced individual with her finger firmly on the pulse in her senior pastoral role. She is also alarmed at the world that has been created for them, both inside and outside the school environment.

We should all be nudged out of complacency when figures in the UK show that suicide amongst 20+ males has risen some 400 per cent in the last 10 years and liver damage due to alcohol and drug abuse in 19-year olds is now a serious problem; and these worrying trends are mirrored throughout all modern societies.

So I also write this book as a concerned member of that feckless society. I realise that as my post-war, baby-boom generation stumbles towards retirement, we need happy, purposeful, well-integrated young people to take on the reins and probably clear up some of our mess.

The third prompting comes from my working experience. I have been a teacher in a variety of schools, and have taught children of all ages and abilities, in schools of all types, including a grammar school, various comprehensives, middle and primary schools. I have also taught in a 'special' unit for 12–16 year olds who had been excluded from their mainstream schools. These youngsters displayed severe behavioural, emotional and learning problems.

I remember my early days in the latter establishment, when a senior educational official visited us, unannounced, one afternoon. He observed me talking to a group of students, before approaching us to ask where the teacher was. At first, I thought perhaps my unsuspected youthfulness had camouflaged me amongst the six or so 15-year-olds. However, my joy was short lived as a pupil suggested that I was 'as crazy as the rest of us, so 'e couldn't tell the difference!' Such moments lightened a frequently difficult task.

My work in therapeutics, and perhaps most relevant here, the teaching of stress management, relaxation and meditational skills, has also prompted this book. I teach such skills each year to groups of young people in local upper (13–18) schools, along with those individuals who, for one reason or another, are either brought or sent by their parents to see me. Few weeks go by without an enquiry from a concerned parent sometimes referred to me by a school who knows of this aspect of my work. And sometimes, though rarer, the student takes the initiative.

The simple techniques in this book are based upon my experience. They are not exclusive and I am sure there are equally good ones that I have omitted. However, these are tried and tested, and if you use them regularly, they will work for you. They will help you to cope with any situation, any test, exam or interview, and what's more, increase your imagination and creativity. As one young 14-year-old boy said to me, 'I feel more in charge, in control now.'

Introduction

My older son, who initially found his advanced level sixth form studies very difficult, having to repeat a year, went from being a failed, unhappy student to achieving very good A level grades and gaining a place at a good university. Whilst initially feeling that what his father did was a bit naff and irrelevant, he eventually asked for my help. The meditation techniques, in particular, he found most useful. He has also used them to good effect in his end of year exams at university, sometimes sending faxes to me whilst I was working overseas asking for clarification about a certain approach or technique we had practised together some time earlier.

Many other youngsters have responded in similar ways and that fills me with much joy and confidence for the future.

Because I am fundamentally an optimist (that is my main prompting), I very much believe in the talents and gifts of everyone and especially young people; you are the future of the western world in particular, and more broadly, the planet.

This book and its ideas are simple, and they are designed to help you to flourish, to achieve, to reach the stars that are there for you to reach. They are to help you experience a sense of purpose and happiness, and maybe a little peace of mind so that you can really be the person you are destined to be.

We shall look at relaxation and meditation techniques – they need practice, but the practice will pay off many times over. We shall also consider other skills for interviews and exams, and simple ways to make your memory a little more effective. We shall consider one or two methods for releasing the anger, fear and frustrations that tend to surround us so that we can feel and be calm in any situation. And calmness means control and effectiveness.

I suggest you have a general read of the book, first of all, and then work through all the key exercises. These are the core exercises I believe we should all do, whoever we are.

The rest are a little more discretionary and rather up to you. I emphasise they are mostly simple. I have found that the simple things work best and are often very powerful in their effect. Get a notebook to accompany your working through this book – it will be most useful.

I believe we are all important. I know you are very important. This book is for you. I hope these pages serve you well and help you.

Paul Lambillion
Bury St Edmunds

Chapter 1
Making Space – Taking Charge

In this first part, consider a few simple ideas that shape your life and largely determine the quality of the experience you have as an individual.

The first is that mentioned in the chapter title, making space – the space to pause, to clear the mind and think freely.

In today's world, we are all surrounded by an ever-increasing range of demands upon our attention. In some ways we can view this as a good thing perhaps. It increases our options and our choices. It makes life more varied and interesting, and, as the saying goes, 'variety is the spice of life'. The more things there are, the more diverse and interesting life can be.

Choices

I have a friend who used to live in Eastern Germany before the fall of Communism and the unification of East and West Germany in the late 1980s. She had never travelled out of the communist block of countries before this time. She was a young woman and remembers the limited choices, if any, she had been able to make as an East German citizen. Many choices, particularly in relation to education, health care, and sport were made for her. She tended to have what food she could get. There were no supermarket shelves loaded with products, as we had become accustomed to in the West since the Second World War. You took whatever was available, bread some days, meat on others and so on.

She also remembers her first visit to the Western part of Germany which was then very prosperous, the third most successful national economy in the world. She told me how she was overwhelmed by what she saw. Not just one type of car, like the old Trabant which was about the only car you would usually see in the East, but Mercedes, Audi, Opel, Ford, Fiat and many others.

In one shop, one of the first she visited, she panicked, and had to leave and go out into the street for a while. She needed to calm down, clear her dizzy head and take stock of things for a moment.

The choice and range of goods bewildered her. She had never seen anything like it, and briefly, she couldn't cope. For her, for a moment, there was simply too much to take in. Gradually, of course, she adjusted, as we all do usually, when we meet a new situation. She learned to cope and to manage her new world, eventually coming to live in the Western part of the new Germany, near Cologne, where I met her.

You have probably grown up in a world where you are used to having choice, used to the many demands made upon you. You are almost certainly accustomed to making choices and doing so consistently.

However, the fact is that every time we have to make a

choice, to engage with the range of products, services and activities that surround us, we use energy – mental, emotional and physical energy.

First of all we consider the choice. We survey what is before us. We may not be conscious of this process, as it is managed subconsciously, but that is what we do. We use our eyes and all our senses to scan what we see before us. It is a conditioned reflex we have learned, engaging our minds, our thoughts in any situation.

The more choice there is, the more scanning there is to do and the more mental energy, or thought power we use in the process. At the same time, we stimulate our emotions and our feelings as we explore the choices.

'I would look good in that.'

or

'What a holiday that could be!'

or

'I bet that tastes brilliant!'

or equally

'Yuk! I'm not wearing that!'

or

'What a dump that looks like!'

or

'I must try that out – wonder what it feels like!'

We observe, and make judgements, and our feelings start to colour our observations. We literally 'colour our judgement'.

Some things will attract us. Some will repel us. And some things will probably have a neutral impact. We feel indifferent to them.

This process uses emotional energy as we consider the

implications of the choice we may make with more questions:

'Can I afford it?'
'Dare I go there?'
'What will people think of me wearing one of those?'

The last question is a significant one. Whoever we are, we are always, to some degree, self-conscious and sensitive to the opinions and reactions of others, whether it's our parents, and the 'olds' generally, our brothers and sisters, neighbours, and perhaps most significantly when we are young, our peer group, school friends, fellow students, boyfriends or girlfriends and so on. Sometimes it's not cool, not acceptable to be seen with or without certain things: CDs, cigarettes, booze, hairstyle, make-up, whatever.

And the making and pursuing of any choice also uses physical energy. Quite apart from the obvious – going to the shops, trailing around (even if you enjoy shopping, it is still physically tiring), choosing the goods, trying them on, taking them home – every time we invoke our thoughts with their feelings and emotions, as we do with any choice, we use up some of our physical energy too.

Muscle Response Test

There is a simple exercise, called a muscle test, that you can try out with a friend, to show how a thought and its accompanying feeling affects your physical energy levels.

1. Stand upright with your arms down beside your body. Slowly raise one arm upwards, keeping it straight, with the palm of your hand facing downwards, towards the floor, until it is level with your shoulder.
2. Ask your friend to then try to push your raised arm back

downwards, using just the tips of their first and second fingers of one hand, whilst you gently resist the attempt to move your arm. Try this for a few seconds and note how effectively you can resist your friend's attempt. Of course, the relative strengths of each of you will be an important factor in this exercise. However, it is not a competition. It is merely a measurement of resistance. Your arm will probably move downwards a little as your friend pushes. Maybe it will move considerably, especially as your arm tires. There will be some resistance, whatever happens.

3. Relax and pause for a moment. Then repeat the process again, raising your arm to shoulder level.
4. This time, use your imagination. Try to think of something you find a little challenging, for example how you feel when you take an examination. Or maybe you can think of something you have done that made you a little anxious. Try not to choose anything too heavy, or frightening, just something challenging. Build the picture in your imagination as vividly as you can.
5. As you think and feel this idea, ask your friend to repeat the attempt to carefully, yet firmly push your arm downwards by pressing on the back of your hand with two fingers.
6. If you keep the thought carefully in your mind, both you and your friend will notice a difference this time. You will find your resistance less effective. The negative thinking and feeling pattern will have used up more of your energy and weakened your resistance.

It may take a couple of attempts before you get the hang of it, but you will notice the difference. When you have finished this test, clear the challenging thought and feeling from your mind.

You can equally try the muscle test to measure a constructive or positive thought and warm emotion or feeling. On this occasion you proceed as before, testing the resistance in your arm in a normal resting state. However, this time, instead of a negative or challenging thought, you do the opposite. Think of how strong you are. Imagine your arm to be strong, almost made of steel. Keep strong, happy, powerful thoughts in your mind. Think to yourself, 'I am strong, powerful, and happy.'

Your friend will notice a difference: this time the resistance will not be weakened. It will almost certainly be greater and so it will be more difficult to push your arm downwards.

It may take a couple of attempts to practise the test, but eventually you will be able to tell the difference. This is one illustration of the way in which your thoughts and feelings also affect your body and its strength and energy.

Key Exercise: Your Mental Suitcase

1. A good way to clear any negative or unpleasant thought is again by using your imagination. We will return to this idea later in the book, but for now, close your eyes and imagine the challenging thought and feeling as if it is written on a piece of paper. See it in your mind as clearly as you can.
2. Then, imagine that next to you there is a large old suitcase. You open the suitcase, and put the piece of paper inside, closing the lid and locking the case securely. You have cleared that feeling and the thought

that brought it to you, out from your mind. Open your eyes slowly when you have closed your suitcase. You will use that suitcase again later on.

Of course, we are meant to learn how to deal with choices. We can't change the world we live in, at least not straight away, so we have to make sure we are equipped with the calmness of mind to choose carefully and with considered judgement. We learn from the choices we make and the effects they have on us. But with calmness, 'staying cool', as my sons would say to me, we can make the best choices and not be pressured into doing, saying, being, or having anything that in our hearts we would rather not have for ourselves.

The key techniques we will go through together will help you to do this.

Making Space

One thing you should consider at this point is making the space in your life to clear your mind so that you can think clearly and in an uncluttered way.

There are many things that impinge on your space and may crowd in on you at times. If you are a student, at school, college or some other institution, or perhaps working and training at the same time, you meet many demands.

Education

There are the demands of your education, with which I am sure you are very familiar, and the expectations that spring from it. Of course, you are certainly capable of achieving whatever you need to achieve; to experience the success necessary for your fulfilment in life. But the demands are there and require a large chunk of your time, and your mental, emotional and physical energy.

Employment
There are the demands of any work you may do. Most young people and students tend to have jobs of some kind and it is good to have them. They are good experience and help us to grow, gain confidence, learn life skills, and perhaps more significantly, they give a little important economic and financial independence and freedom.

Friends and Relationships
Our friends and family are important to us. Yours are important to you. We probably learn most through those we come into contact with in our lives, our parents, brothers and sisters, grandparents, aunts and uncles, school and college pals, teachers and others. We learn both from those we like and those we don't like much. But all our encounters are of benefit to us and help us to develop our interpersonal skills. We learn how to handle people.

Perhaps most of all, we learn from our intimate relationships, our boyfriends or girlfriends, husbands/wives and partners. All these relationships are important for us and falling in love is a wonderful, if at times, painful experience, not to be missed. But sometimes, it can be difficult for many of us to have space from others. You may live in a house full of family, attend a school or college with many pupils and have many friends. You may have colleagues at work too. We all need space on our own.

Making Space – Taking Charge

TV, Radio, Telephones

Count the number of telephones in your house. In ours, there are six when everyone is at home from university and so on: two landlines and four mobiles. There is also email and the Internet. Mobile phones are an asset when used wisely. But, like all telephones, they ring and make demands on us. 'Answer me!' or 'Text me!' they say and whether we want to or not, they demand our attention. A mobile is a permanent link to others which can be intrusive when out of control. Mine is switched off most of the time, but if you have a mobile, it is another source of demand upon you, your attention, your time and subsequently your energies. And of course, TV and radio are difficult to get away from. They can be great fun, but they present much choice, more than ever before, to you and everyone. They make demands on us and push their way into our space.

Music

A word here about music. I love music. I have sung professionally and with a rock band in the 1960s. My sons and my daughter have large collections of CDs covering a broad range of music. Music can be very calming and emotionally healing. It can be inspiring. However, some contemporary music is a particular stimulus and it literally winds us up and excites us. It is meant to do that and, for some of the time, that's great and worthwhile fun. Listen to a variety of music and take time to have music free time also.

Later, when we consider memory and revision approaches before exams, we will see how certain styles of music can aid the assimilation of ideas and information. Noise is generally tiring. It has been proven to impact on us

Staying Cool

and eventually cause fatigue. Sometimes we adjust to it and our mind filters it out for us. People who live near to a busy road, or railway track, for example, usually stop hearing the noise after a while and it no longer disturbs them, but incessant noise is wearing. It is good and beneficial to have quiet sometimes.

Key Exercise: Taking a Pause

At this point, if you do not do so already, introduce a pause into your day. A time where you just simply stop, drop everything and everyone. This can be done when you get home from school, college or work.

1. Turn off anything that may disturb you: mobile phone, TV, radio. Stick a 'post-it' on the door and write on it *Taking a Pause*. Sit down for a few moments alone. Close your eyes. (Closing your eyes immediately slows everything down.)
2. Imagine your mental suitcase, the one you used earlier. Unlock it, open it and put into it everything that has occupied your mind so far during the day, especially all the things that, for one reason or another, have weighed on your mind. Imagine them written down on pieces of paper, which you now place in your suitcase one at a time. If they are important, you can take them out again later and deal with them then, as you choose to.
3. For now, shut them in the case, close the case and lock the lid down.
4. Just for a few minutes, simply think to yourself: 'I am taking a pause.' And then be quiet. You do not have to do this for long. A few minutes will be fine. It will be a very valuable two or three minutes. Your heart rate will

slow down a little. Any tensions will start to ease, both in your body and in your mind.
5. Enjoy the experience. Then open your eyes slowly and take a further moment or two to reflect on your plans for the rest of the day, and what you wish or need to do next. Then you can spring into action!

If you are tired, you may well nod off for a few minutes and that's fine. This pause is so important to take and we should all make a practice of taking it from time to time. It is not only that you are taking a rest simply by not doing anything – a difficult proposition in a world that encourages us all to be busy all the time, 'going for it!', and if we're not busy we are either lazy or missing out on something. You often hear this type of conversation:

Questioner: 'How are things?'
Reply: 'Oh, I'm so busy these days! Life is frantic, so full.'
Questioner: 'Great!'

But if the reply had been as follows: 'Oh, I'm quiet. Things are calm and going along gently,' I feel the response might have been somewhere between a patronising 'Well I suppose that's good if you like it like that,' to an 'Oh dear', implying that frantic and busy are the only modes of living that are of any value. However, 'busy' doesn't mean dynamic or purposeful, or thorough or efficient, or fulfilling and enjoyable. Some of the time, maybe, but not all the time.

What perhaps is equally important about your pause is the fact that you are briefly banning intrusions. You are actually taking control, taking charge of your life's rhythm and choosing to slow it down for a while.

If you use nothing else from this book, other than

introduce a pause or two into your day, your mind and body will benefit from it. That I can assure you.

Changing Pace and Rhythm

We are more effective as people if we learn to change the pace of our lives, to alter the rhythm of things and build into it some variety, some contrasts. Changes of pace in our lives help us to become more adaptable, more able to encounter new experiences, explore them more confidently, develop new talents and be open to fresh thoughts and ideas. This is essential for the solving of problems, and to feeling in control, come what may.

In the busy, fast-moving world in which you live, such changes are essential. As little children, we tend to keep going, bubbling with energy until we drop and collapse in a heap, only to recover and then explode into activity again. As we grow, we learn that this is not the best use of our energy. We learn to pace ourselves, to vary the pace of things.

A Review of Your Life Rhythm

An interesting exercise is to take a moment or two to look at your life and reflect upon it.

Just run your mind through a typical week and look at how it fits together. Look at all the aspects of it and the balance between work, rest and leisure. You are not here seeking to make a value judgement, to decide what is good or bad.

Just look at the pattern. Inevitably, work, whether in the form of school, study or a job, will occupy the most significant chunk of your time. That's how it is for most of

Making Space – Taking Charge

us, short of winning the National Lottery. And anyway, we all need structured, creative activity. Also, when we are young, especially, we like to make sure we 'play' and have leisure time that is enjoyable. Quite right too! When I was at school and during my college years, I enjoyed a good social and sporting life and my own children are certainly like their father in that respect.

But perhaps the most neglected side tends to be the resting bit. Not only do we need substantial, if slightly differing hours of sleep, we also need conscious pauses, moments to slow down and restore our bodies and clear our minds. So view the three areas and look to see what, if anything, seems to be neglected.

Ask yourself these questions:
1. 'Am I giving sufficient time and energy to my work, my studies, my education?'
2. 'Do I take sufficient space to relax and have good and varied social activity?'

    Some of us are more social than others, but we all need time away from work that is active and creative in its own right. The more varied your leisure is, the better. You will have your hobbies, or preferences, but try not to get stuck in a rut in your leisure time.
3. 'Am I having sufficient rest and sleep and taking space to re-charge my batteries?'

    Here you need to make sure you get enough sleep. When we are young, especially, early nights can seem a nuisance. The English comedian, the late Terry Scott, dressed up as a rather old-fashioned schoolboy, would sing, 'Why do parents send me to bed when I'm wide awake, and wake me up when I'm still tired?' So get your sleep. You can usually tell what your own optimum sleep time is, but in busy lives, in periods of accelerated physical growth (adolescence) and in times of great demand (examinations, and times of intensive study and learning) we tend to need a little more than usual.

We will consider this balance in the later chapters of this book. For now, look to creating space simply for clearing your mind. Such things as yoga and Tai chi can help, but some pause and mental relaxation and meditational technique is also vital.

Where you spot an imbalance in your life rhythm or feel the need to make a change, do so. Even write it down somewhere and commit yourself to having a balanced life, a happy blend of work, rest, and leisure.

Stillness, Thinking and Creativity

People often come up with interesting ideas in remarkable and sometimes unusual situations. The reason is that when we pause, and take some space, we allow ourselves to be open to thoughts and ideas that are blocked when we are busy, caught up in a frantic life.

Sometimes it can be when we go to bed that we are touched by a new idea, an original thought or even the solution to a problem. J.K. Rowling, author of the Harry Potter books, was travelling on a train when the ideas for the stories came to her and she then had to find some paper to write them down as they entered her mind in quick succession. The basis for the Harry Potter stories was born.

When we look at memory and taking examinations

later on in this book, we will consider this idea and how we can access thoughts and ideas. They include those stored in our minds from our previous experience and learning, and those new, creative ideas that we can access as we need them. This is where pausing and stillness is such an important idea.

Your Mental Filing Cabinet

Your mind is remarkable. It continually absorbs information from your experience; from what you see, hear, feel and touch, smell and taste.

Whatever you experience, it is recorded in your mind, most commonly by the camera effect in your eyes, or the recording of the sounds you hear. From when we are small, we also learn to recognise and remember things by scent and by taste. The sense of touch is important too, especially in our early years. As we get older, it is our hearing and seeing which tend to dominate, but of course, all our senses are important and useful in recording and processing our experience, and then providing whatever information we need to take action and be creative in our lives.

You Never Forget

One important thing to remember is that our mind registers everything we see, hear, and experience. Of course, some things make a greater impact on us than others do, and so the memory is perhaps more vivid, more powerful and therefore more accessible, easier to get at in our minds if we wish to recall it. This is because our powerful experiences, those events that make a great impact on us, whether pleasant or unpleasant, summon up vivid pictures and sensations as we recall them, accompanied by strong, powerful feelings. The nature of the feeling qualifies the experience; in other words, it tells us whether we liked the experience or not, whether it was happy or sad, stirring or calming, and so on.

I remember vividly some powerful experiences from my past, for example being stuck, on my own, in the ghost train at a seaside fairground because my train broke down, right in front of an illuminated spook! I was eight at the time and will never forget it! Fortunately, I can also remember thoughts that summon up happy feelings and good memories.

> **The key idea here is that you never, ever, forget anything. Everything you experience makes an imprint in your mind and is with you for the rest of your life.**

It is true that injuries and shocks of various types can block out memories, sometimes to protect us from the trauma involved. My daughter can never remember the serious car accident in which she was involved, although I can personally remember nearly dying when hit by lightning as a boy!

But everything we encounter we place in the filing cabinet of our mind. The down side of this is that minds can become cluttered, even confused, usually because we try to cram too much in at once, and don't give ourselves the pauses and space needed to process things and file them away properly.

Making Space – Taking Charge

The positive side is that if you give yourself regular pauses, you not only help your mind to assimilate and file away your experiences properly, you also create a tidier filing system in your mind, enabling better and quicker access to what you need from your memories, your experience.

Moments of stillness and regular pauses help us to process our experiences, store them away tidily, and access them effectively as we wish to. You forget nothing, you simply lose access to it.

Creating a Mental Filing Cabinet

1. Think of your mind as a huge, massive, filing cabinet. It is full of drawers. Build a picture of this in your imagination: a large filing cabinet full of drawers.
2. Everything you have ever experienced is recorded somewhere in your mind. It is filed away in your mind's filing system. You can access it whenever you wish to. You may need to practise this access, but access it you can. You can recall anything you have seen, read, heard and experienced. Each drawer in your filing cabinet is labelled, showing you what is inside.
3. You can look down the drawers of your filing cabinet. There is a drawer for everything. Seek out the label you are looking for. It can be anything, 'Addresses', 'Dates', 'Telephone Numbers', 'Historical Notes' or 'Scientific Facts', and so on.
4. Imagine yourself looking for the appropriate drawer and read the label on the outside. When you find the one that is appropriate, open it and then look for the appropriate file. The file will have a little label on it with the name or title of what you are looking for.

5. Find the file, lift it out and open it. Words and pictures will begin to form. Be patient and give it time. You will be able to find what you are looking for, even if it takes a little practice. We will look at ways of storing information in your mind later on. The important idea to emphasise here is: *You never forget anything.*

You may misplace it for a while, forgetting where you put it, but: *You never forget anything.*

By introducing pauses and moments of stillness, you will improve your memory and develop your creativity. It is in moments of stillness that you unclutter and organise your mind, allowing yourself the space to be creative.

A young artist came to see me some time ago. He was very talented, but he had experienced a lot of problems in his life and he felt very uncreative and uninspired. His mind was cluttered and confused, and his normal creativity was blocked off, because he hadn't filed everything away properly. By using a number of the techniques in this book, he cleared away some of the mental junk that was confusing him; he became calmer and his creativity gradually returned to him.

When we take time to be still, our mind has a chance to order itself, sort itself out and a door opens in us, a door to the creative imagination. The ideas will then just flow again. Little pauses, moments of stillness, help the uncluttering of our minds and open the door in us to clearer thinking and greater creativity.

Henry Ford, inventor of the Ford motor car, was reputed to have a good mental filing system. Whenever he hit a problem, he would file it away in his mind, putting it on the back-burner, and he would return to it later when he had cleared his mind and made space for new ideas to come to him. It served him well.

The little pauses help to clear the clutter from your mind and make you more creative, more imaginative.

The Open and Closed Mind

We seldom control our thinking, and even when we do, it is usually in short bursts followed by a period of chaos. To a certain extent this is okay as there are two major modes of mind.

The Open Mode

This is when we are very creative, for example when we are painting a picture, writing a story, or using our imagination to come up with new ideas and fresh perspectives, a new way of seeing things.

We are very creative in this open mode. We are like an unwritten book waiting for new ideas to come into our minds. It is very important, and in a busy world, frequently neglected. We are often chastised at work or at school for not doing anything, for pausing to stare out of the window for a few moments, or to reflect. I was often accused of day dreaming at school, and whilst I accept it is not good to daydream all the time, it is an essential part of a balanced, creative mind.

It is a foolish teacher (or boss) who chastises someone for 'not working' when what the person is really doing is thinking. Without some space to be in this open mode, we are never likely to function as effectively as we could. We won't reach our true potential, whatever we are working at, at the time.

The Closed Mode

This is the time when we have solved the problem, or come up with an idea, and then seek to do something with it, to make our ideas practical, to make them work.

In the closed mode, we process our ideas, narrow them down, and seek practical solutions to our problems, or find how to proceed with a task. We implement the plan we have, or we organise the facts before we use them.

Your mind is in a constant movement from *open* to *closed* and back to *open*. It is your creative process. It makes it possible for you to bring all your knowledge and ideas into your mind, then apply them as clearly and effectively as you can.

Open mode – ideas flood in.

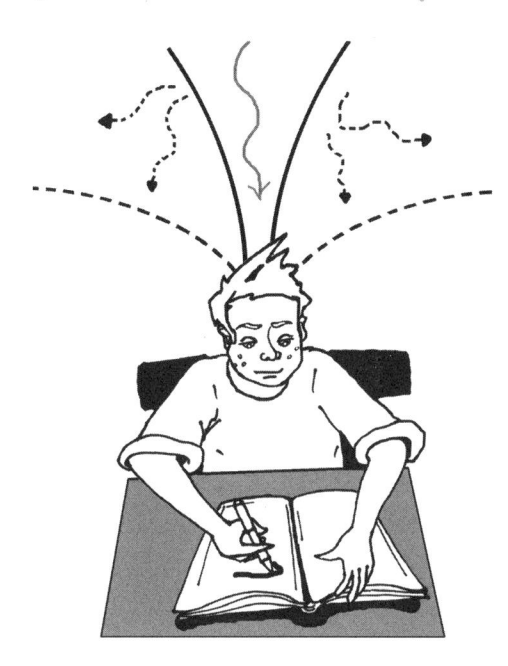

Closed mode – organising an idea.

We need both modes:
- Open mode – the space to gain access to our thoughts, ideas and stored knowledge
- Closed mode – the ordering of these thoughts, ideas and information, so we can use them in a task, e.g. an examination, essay, a painting.

In the open mode we pause, reflect, and access information.

In the closed mode we organise the information we have recalled, the original ideas we have had, and then use them in whichever way we choose.

When we learn and use the correct balance between these two modes of thinking, we can flourish and be very creative and imaginative, whether we are writing an essay and organising facts, or solving a problem, maybe in maths or science, or in a practical situation like painting, writing music, or making something.

Candle Gazing

This is a very good way to calm down and begin to learn how to control your thinking. There is something magical and soothing about candlelight. So for this exercise, find a small candle. Make sure it is firmly fixed into a stable candle holder and placed safely where you can see it and watch it. Place a saucer or plate underneath it and make sure that it is away from anything flammable. To benefit from this exercise, try to ensure you will not be disturbed for a few moments. Light your candle and then sit quietly, looking at the candle's flame.

1. Go to your imaginary suitcase, open the lid and put into it any thoughts or concerns you may have, or that stray into your mind. You can deal with them later on, as and when it is appropriate to do so.
2. Focus your attention upon the candle flame. Observe it and keep your attention upon it. If you are tired, your eyes may wish to close, but try to keep your attention on the flame. Study it as if you are going to describe it to someone afterwards: how still, bright and clear it looks and what colours you can see in it.
3. Other thoughts will inevitably seek to flow through your mind and grab your attention. If and when they do, simply pause for a moment, put them into your mental suitcase, and then return to your candle and observe its flame. Whatever thoughts you have, keep with the ones

that relate to the candle and its flame. The others you can put into your suitcase as they arise.
4. Practise this, initially for about five minutes. You will get better and better at it. You will find that stray, random thoughts will crowd into your mind less and less often. You can also extend your gazing to ten minutes if you wish to.

You will notice that the exercise becomes easier and easier, and you will find that, the more you practise, the easier it is to concentrate upon the candlelight.

This is a simple beginning in controlling your thinking and, at the same time, calming your mind. A calm mind is a clear mind. And a clear mind is creative and effective. You will have made a good start to becoming more effective, more successful and staying clear and cool in any situation.

You are making space and taking charge.

Summary of Activities

- *Muscle Response Test*

Try the muscle response test for viewing the way your body reacts to thoughts and feelings and how your thoughts affect your energy and strength.

- *Key Exercise: Your Mental Suitcase*

Use your imagination to make a mental suitcase. Put into this suitcase any thoughts or ideas that are interfering with your concentration or focus at any time, whether it is in a lesson, a lecture, when reading or writing, painting or whatever. In this way, you begin to select what you think about. This is especially important when taking a pause. Important things or issues, you can deal with later on. You will not forget them if you need them. They are in your suitcase and that is in your mind.

- *Key Exercise: Taking a Pause*

Put a 'pause' into your day, a moment where you simply stop, put everything down, and make some space to be still and quiet, without noise or distractions.

- *A Review of Your Life Rhythm*

From time to time, look at your life rhythm, especially the relationship between *work, rest* and *leisure.*

- *Creating a Mental Filing Cabinet*

Remember your mind is like a huge, mental filing cabinet where everything you have experienced is filed away for future reference.

- *Candle Gazing*

Try a little slowing down and concentration by occasional, five-minute candle gazing. (Always put your candle in a safe place and extinguish it when you have finished!)

Chapter 2
Stress and Relaxation

The word *stress* is often used these days, and the inevitable consequence is that we cease to really understand what it means. In fact, without some stress, there is no adequate tension for the release of energy. Without some stress, we cannot function properly at all.

An example of this is the archer, with his bow and arrow. To fire the arrow, the archer must pull back the bowstring, with the arrow in place, providing the optimum degree of tension before its release, allowing the arrow to fly off to its target. Insufficient tension or stress, and the arrow will hardly travel anywhere; too much, and the bowstring or bow may well snap. And if he never releases the tension, the string gets tighter and tighter, and then weaker and weaker. The same happens with our own tension and stress.

I have done some work with a number of athletes, sports men and women, one of whom recently excelled, achieving victories and gold medals internationally, when most thought he could no longer do so. The next time there is an athletics meeting on your TV, or a swimming race, or tennis match, observe the participants.

Staying Cool

In order to perform effectively, they have to achieve this fine balance between stress and relaxation; to be relaxed as and when is necessary, but also to summon up just the appropriate tensions and stresses necessary to run the race, make the dive or hit the racket. I heard a commentator recently, watching Greg Rudsedski, the British tennis player, playing against Pete Sampras in the American Open Tournament. Rudsedski was playing well, when suddenly he seemed to 'tighten up'. His tennis strokes and shots lost their earlier flow when he had been winning the game, and he was now snatching at his shots, putting them either too short and hitting the net, or too long and out of the court. He was becoming too tense, too stressed and losing the necessary balance between tension and relaxation.

Stress and Relaxation

It is a fine balance, one we all need to reach and experience if we are to truly express ourselves and realise our greatest potential in our lives. In sport, a fraction too much tension can lead to losing a point in a tennis set, crashing into the hurdle in a race, or hitting a shot over the bar in a soccer match.

The same is true in all walks of life and in all activities. Too much stress and our minds go blank; we may even panic. Too little, and we may lack the alertness, energy and dynamism necessary to succeed.

Unfortunately, in modern Western society, overstressing, or excessive unreleased tension is a real and common problem. We 'tighten our bows' but frequently don't release the string fully. We build up and accumulate stress in our system. Eventually, the bow won't fire any arrows, and we don't function properly anymore. Our minds become cluttered, our bodies become less efficient, and even our immune system suffers. It is common for people experiencing excessive or unfamiliar levels of stress to develop head colds, minor infections, headaches and so on. There are now volumes of research that indicate that our mental and emotional state affects our bodies. The very term psychosomatic, sometimes used incorrectly to suggest that an illness is imaginary and therefore unreal, means 'mind and body' and underlines the idea that the mind affects the body.

Mind over Matter

You can test this for yourself in a simple way. I have been using the techniques in this book for over twenty years and know their effects on the lives of those, both students and non-student young people, that I have worked with. This test is another simple indicator for you.

Staying Cool

The Lemon
1. Sit quietly and close your eyes for a few moments.
2. Using your imagination, picture in front of you a fresh ripe lemon and a small sharp knife.
3. Imagine the lemon as clearly as you can, its colour, its shiny yellow skin and its slightly bobbly, uneven surface.
4. Now, in your mind, see the lemon being cut, revealing its juicy inside of fleshy, yellow segments.
5. Next, imagine picking up one piece of the lemon, and bringing it to your lips, feel yourself to be sucking some of the juice. As you do this, notice what happens in your mouth. You may well be surprised at the reaction!

There used to be an old joke, years ago, that you could seriously impair the ability of a trumpet player, as he played his trumpet, if you sucked a lemon in front of him. Upon seeing the lemon, he would switch in his mind to his memory of its bitter, sharp taste, and be unable to purse his lips adequately to blow through the trumpet's mouthpiece. (I'm not suggesting you do this in a concert!) Your mind will remind you of the lemon's taste and your mouth will respond accordingly.

Delicious Food
1. You can try the same thing again, only this time, imagine something you really find tasty, something you find delicious to eat.
2. Build a good picture in your mind again. Bring it up to your mouth and bite into it.
3. Notice how your saliva glands will run freely in your mouth, even though there is no real food there, only the

idea, the image or the thought. Your mouth will really 'water' if you build a vivid picture.

My dog has a very good mind response to some food and the pleasure it brings to her! She has a great love of apples and she will sit in front of me whilst I am eating one, dribbling profusely, hoping that a morsel might fall her way. She has a good memory, and a good imagination which affects the working of her digestive system. If it is true for her, it is certainly true for you.

In both these cases, you were merely thinking, quite briefly, of the idea. And your body responded. Your thoughts affect your body chemistry quite clearly.

Here is another 'mind over matter' technique you can try, to show how you can influence your body's response with a thought or an idea. This is a good one to try on a friend, parent, or teacher!

Rubberneck

1. Sit upright, facing to the front, with your hands resting upon your lap.
2. Very slowly, turn your head to one side, as far as you possibly can, whilst remaining comfortable, keeping your chest to the front.
3. Find a visual reference point to measure how far you have managed to turn your head. It may be an object of some kind or a mark on the wall, or whatever.
4. Slowly, return your face to the front and relax for a moment.
5. Now, use your imagination again. Imagine that your neck is made of very flexible, bendy rubber. Build a

picture in your mind of a very springy, flexible rubber neck. Imagine what that would feel like, how easy it would be to move your head.

6. Open your eyes again, and turn your head slowly in the same direction as before, as far as you can without hurting your neck in any way. This time, you will find that you can move your head more, albeit fractionally so, and look further around than before, beyond your earlier reference point or object. Slowly, return your face to the front.

Of course, different people will experience differing degrees of response to these tests, but it is not a competition. You will certainly notice a response in one, if not all of them, if you try them. It illustrates in a simple way what science has been forced to acknowledge in research in recent times: our thoughts directly affect our responses and our body functions.

This is not a new idea; in fact it is a very old one. In a publication as long ago as 1870, a famous British doctor, Sir James Paget, expressed a belief that mental distress was an important factor in the development of serious physical illness.

Dr Herbert Benson, a renowned researcher at the Harvard University Medical School in America, found that deep mental relaxation could lower blood pressure, and not only during the relaxation period, but also in the period afterwards, sustained excessively high blood pressure being one common symptom of excessive, continual over-stressing.

Our accumulated stress takes away from us many good things. If we don't take space to relax properly, clear our minds, quieten down and pause, then we are limiting our effectiveness and storing up problems for later on. And in our busy world, we have to re-educate ourselves to relax and make the best use of the gifts and talent we have.

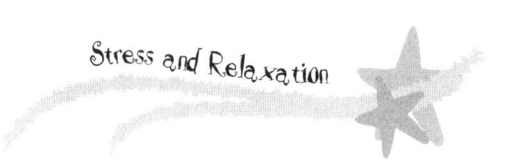

Before we go any further, we will consider a simple unstressing and relaxation technique. This is really the first part of a process that you will find invaluable and will, if practised regularly, gradually release stresses, both those that have accumulated in you over a period of time and also those that you will meet on a day-to-day basis. Instead of carrying them around like an ever-increasing, and largely hidden burden, this process will safely and gently unfold them for you, ultimately preventing you from ever being over-stressed again.

Unstressing Yourself 1

This exercise develops 'Taking a pause' from the last chapter with some basic relaxation activity. It is still useful to take a short pause from time to time, to take a few moments of stillness and quietness, not only at the end of the day, but in odd, free moments, when one activity or task is completed, and before you start another. Frequent, brief pauses are a good way to clear the mind and release stress, thus increasing your energy levels.

Now, however, I suggest you develop your major pause, the time you will give, at least once a day, to developing a process for unstressing. It is best done either at the beginning of your day, before breakfast and major daily activity or, probably most convenient for some, at the end of the day, either late afternoon or early evening, just before your evening meal. Try to practise this before eating as a simple breathing technique is involved. A full stomach may make you drowsy, and also it makes it more difficult for your diaphragm to stretch your lungs downwards, filling them with oxygen, energising your bloodstream, calming your nervous system as it does so.

If you are really diligent, twice a day is even better. The benefits are immense and I do not need to re-iterate that anything worth doing needs an investment of time and commitment. You are investing in yourself here, your own best asset.

Posture
1. Sit upon a comfortable, upright chair, with your feet touching the floor.
2. Make sure you will not be disturbed for a few moments. Tell other people in the house what you are doing, switch off your mobile phone, and turn off anything else that may distract you.
3. Rest your hands on your lap and loosen any clothing that may feel tight, especially around your waist and neck.

Neck Exercise
We accumulate a lot of physical tension around our necks and shoulders, especially when we spend time writing, drawing and painting, or working a keyboard.
1. To loosen your neck, simply close your eyes. Imagine your head to be a heavy weight (which it is), and slowly allow it to fall sideways, towards your right shoulder, as far as it will go comfortably. Your neck may creak and crackle a bit. That's quite natural.
2. Allow your head to rest on or near to your right shoulder for a slow count of five and then gradually move it back

into the upright position. Imagine you are 'lifting' your head back into the upright position and, as you do so, taking the weight off your neck.
3. After a few seconds, slowly lower your head, this time towards your left shoulder, or as far as it will go comfortably. Again, you may hear a few cracks and pops. Allow the weight of your head to rest on or near to the left shoulder, for a slow mental count of five, before returning to the upright position.
4. Remember to do this slowly, and that you 'lift' your head back to the centre again. Then repeat this on both shoulders, once more, releasing the tensions from your neck and shoulders.
5. Finally, move your chin downwards, until it touches or nearly touches your chest. Keep it there for a slow count of five and then 'lift' it slowly back into the upright position. Repeat this once more. Try not to bend your neck forwards as you do this. The idea is to stretch it as you move your chin downwards as far as it goes.

Although this is not a 'key exercise' as such, it is useful to do from time to time as an unwinding technique prior to deep breathing and relaxation.

Key Exercise: Unstressing Yourself 1 – Breathing

1. Sitting quietly, close your eyes and put any unwanted thoughts and ideas into your mental suitcase.
2. Then, take your attention gently downward from your head until you are aware of your solar plexus, or stomach area. The solar plexus is the space just beneath you sternum or breastbone.

Staying Cool

The solar plexus.

Notice how, as you breathe in, your stomach and abdomen rise upwards, and after a pause, they gently move back again, for another pause, before your next inhalation and breathing cycle. Focus on this movement for a few moments as you breathe in and out.

3. As your breath slows and deepens, be aware of the motion of your breath flowing in through your nose (never breathe in through your mouth), filling your lungs as your diaphragm gently stretches your lungs downward towards the bottom of your rib cage. This is a wonderful, remarkable motion that we rather take for granted, and yet which occurs all the time, every day of our lives. When this breath is finished, your diaphragm slowly allows your lungs to contract and so expel the carbon dioxide from your body, squeezing it out as you exhale.

4. As you become more comfortable and aware of this movement, slow your breath down a little more. You can encourage this by one of three methods:

Stress and Relaxation

- Slowly say to yourself in your mind as you breathe *'I – breathe – in – pause'* and – *'I – breathe – out – pause'* and … You may sound a little strange at first, but persevere; it will be well worth doing so.

or

- Simply count slowly as you breathe in *'1 – 2 – 3'* pause for a moment and then *'1 – 2 – 3'* as you exhale, pausing briefly before your next in breath.

I find one or both of the above work for most students, but you can also try this:

- Think of the waves of a calm, gentle sea, rolling gently up and down. Keep this idea in your mind as you focus upon your breathing, and your breath will gradually slow down until you are breathing more slowly in harmony with the waves of the sea and its gentle rising and falling rhythm.

By concentrating on your solar plexus, you will also naturally begin to breathe more deeply, filling your lungs and bloodstream with more oxygen and your

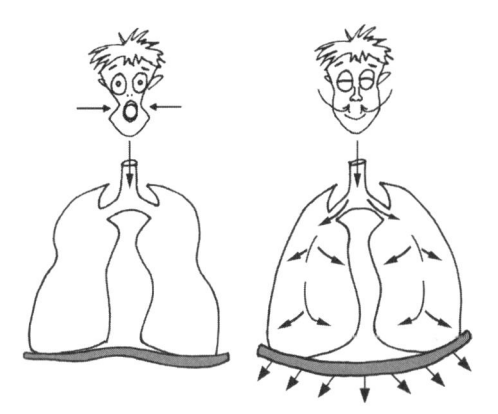

Diaphragm stretches lungs as they fill with air.

body with more energy. Your mind will also begin to calm down and clear. Negative feelings will loosen and float away like white clouds on the summer breeze.

The solar plexus is a large complex of nerves, near to the stomach, which controls much of how we feel and respond. We will discuss the solar plexus a little more later on.

For the moment, practise this exercise for some 5–10 minutes, at least once a day, and twice if you can manage to slot it in. It will be well worth the effort and, even after a few days, you will be aware of the calmness it creates in you and around you.

5. To draw this exercise to a close, simply bring your attention up from your solar plexus, letting go of your breath for now, and focus your attention around your eyes. Then open your eyes slowly, and remain seated for a few moments until you feel fully awakened and alert. 'Ground' yourself by feeling your feet firmly upon the floor, before you get up and go about the rest of your day.

If you find, during the early practising of this exercise, and indeed any exercise in this book, that thoughts and ideas and distractions come into your mind, place them in your mental suitcase, and then gently guide your concentration back to the exercise in hand. You can deal with other things later on if necessary. This time is for your relaxation and unstressing and that is your priority.

After a little practice, you will discover that you can easily slow down your breath, inducing rhythmic, even, deep breathing. It is a programming, and eventually, your subconscious mind will get the message, understand it and switch on as you request it. Think 'deep, rhythmic breathing' and with more practice, that is what you will get.

A 16-year-old girl at one school where I taught these techniques used to panic badly in exams. Like many, she found them difficult, challenging experiences. She had learned to slow down her breathing, making her feel calmer, although she hadn't really practised the exercise for long enough to clear all the panicky feelings she suffered at such times.

During one exam she panicked and had to leave the room. She was hyperventilating, snatching short, shallow breaths, which made her feel faint and weak, unable to concentrate, unable to cope. In such circumstances we absorb insufficient oxygen and use only a tiny part of our lung capacity. She sat in a corridor with a teacher, in an extremely distressed state, and then recalled what I had taught her. She spoke to the teacher between her short breaths, 'I remember what Mr Lambillion taught us. I'm going to do that!' And she did.

She gradually calmed down, got back in control and was able to return to the room and complete her exam. A triumph for her and a wonderful example of how a simple technique can help calm us down and clear a problem. We will develop this technique some more later on. And regular practice will prevent the panics from occurring in the first place.

The Duvet Technique!

You can practise the development of rhythmic breathing anywhere. Before nodding off to sleep, I often lie in bed and breathe slowly and rhythmically. It's a good way to slow down, clear your mind and prepare for deeper, more refreshing sleep.

1. You can practise this also just before you go off to sleep.
2. Lying on your back, breathe slowly and deeply, with those even, rhythmic breaths.
3. Your duvet or bedclothes will rise slowly upwards and then downwards, reflecting your breathing movement as you relax yourself into a good, peaceful night's sleep. Try the duvet technique at the end of your day!

Brain Rhythms and the Alpha State

Today, we are generally aware that our brains function in quite specific rhythms or frequencies, frequencies which are the electrical activity produced as the cells in the brain perform their various tasks. These brain waves or patterns vary both in their strength and their frequency, depending on the specific type of activity we are engaged in at any given moment. We sometimes say 'I've had a brain wave', meaning we've had a really good idea, or a sudden inspiration. Brain waves are measured in cycles per second, called Hertz, usually abbreviated as Hz. When we are in our normal, awakened state, our brain's electrical wave pattern is somewhere between 30 Hertz (Hz) to 13 Hertz (Hz), or 30 to 13 waves per second.

These waves are measured by an instrument known as the electroencephalograph or ECG machine. Electrodes are placed upon the scalp and the machine measures the frequency of the brain, revealing its level of activity and also indicating any unusual patterns which may be indicative of a problem or some disease.

In a normal waking state, our brains register this *Beta*

rhythm at 13–30 Hz. We use this kind of brain activity at this frequency range when we are engaged in our everyday activities, concentrating on particular tasks, or problems, focusing on conversations and on our general interaction with life around us. It is the rhythm of our response to our outer world and daily life. Whilst reading this text, your brain will be mainly in Beta rhythm.

As you quieten down and begin to relax, your brain wave patterns change and slow down also. In fact, as soon as you close your eyes, your brain begins to slow down and show increasingly slower waves, between 13 and 8 Hertz or cycles per second. This is called the *Alpha rhythm* and it is generally considered to be the beginning of relaxation and healing in us. It seems to be the point at which we begin to shut out the outside world, cease to be reactive to everything around us and start to clear our minds. It is that period when we close our eyes, just before the patterns and images begin to form in the picture-making mechanism deep inside our minds. We can slip in and out of this state usually very quickly when our attention is drawn by some outer activity around us, like a sudden loud noise, or something occurring to make us open our eyes, or remind us of a worry or something that has been occupying our thoughts for some time.

This is the threshold of a calmer state, a kind of transition period between being fully awake and entering a deeper healing and highly creative level of awareness. It is for you the doorway to unstressing and greater personal power.

There is a further state of calmness, that of our *Theta rhythm* or brain wave pattern with waves predominantly between 7 and 4 Hertz or cycles per second. You enter this state in a variety of ways, but mainly through deep relaxation and meditation techniques which we are exploring as we go through this book. As you practise the Key Exercises you will go into the Alpha level and establish occasional Theta wave patterns in your brain. It is a profound healing state to experience, both for the rest and repair of your physical body and the clearing of negative emotions you would rather not continue to have, emotions that may impede your mental performance in situations you encounter in your normal, awakened state.

The Alpha/Theta brain waves lead you to a more creative, more imaginative level. A door in your mind opens to original ideas and enables you to reach deep inside so that you can access memory and find the solutions to problems, often giving fresh insights or a different view of an issue. By the regular practising of the techniques for achieving Alpha and Theta levels, you will be more creative and mentally alert, when you return to normal Beta waking activity. The door you have opened stays ajar, and with each relaxation, you open it wider and wider. You also enter Theta just before and after deep sleep and during dreaming. This is why it is always worth having your journal near to your bed at night, so that if you wake with a good idea, you can write it down before you forget it!

The musician and former Beatle Paul McCartney told a story once of how he was commissioned to write the theme music to a big movie. Having spent a little time considering how he might write it, and playing with ideas, he awoke one night from sleep with a tune in his head which was perfect for the project. He went downstairs and recorded it quickly on his keyboard, and within a short time, he had the whole score ready. It had popped up through his mind as his brain moved between Theta and Alpha. If he can do it, so can you. Maybe you won't compose a tune, but you can be original and creative.

Left Brain, Right Brain

There is another important idea here to consider, which helps to explain the effects of calming down and seeking moments of pause and deep relaxation.

It is generally accepted that the two hemispheres of our brain perform very different and essential functions. The left-hand side of your brain is where the intellectual activity takes place. This is the logical part which helps you to work things out in a structured, practical way. It likes order and it helps you to function as a person in 'straight lines', moving logically from one thing to another. It is very connected with the 'closed state' mentioned in the last chapter. The left-hand side of your brain helps you to apply ideas and make them work, for example in mathematics, technology and so on.

Staying Cool

The right-hand side of your brain is the part which accesses and processes ideas; it helps you to be creative, imaginative and original. It allows you to fantasise, and let your mind roam freely, as in daydreaming. Your right brain enables you to be artistic, musical, and poetic as in the 'open' state of mind.

Of course, the most effective people use both hemispheres of the brain equally. In our Western society today, it is considered that we are too left-brain dominant, too logical and too narrow in our thinking. Recently, the UK government created a 'think tank', a group of people to come up with solutions to the increasing problem of traffic on our roads. They called it 'Blue Sky Thinking'. This group was encouraged to come up with new ideas and solutions, using some open right-brain thinking, even if they appeared to be outrageous. Sometimes a good, fresh idea can seem ridiculous or unworkable until, after some good, left-brain thinking and analysis, we find a practical way to apply the idea. This is what inventors and innovators do: they access new ideas and then find ways of making them work.

The difficulty we all face is that, too often, these two hemispheres work independently of each other, like strangers, the one not knowing what the other is doing. Regular, deep relaxation and meditation techniques bring the electrical activity of these two hemispheres closer together until they synchronise and co-operate once again, enabling clearer mental function, improved memory, greater powers and longer periods of concentration and an enhanced ability to make clear decisions and choices.

Creative visualisation, which we will practise, also links these two hemispheres, making us more effective, more balanced.

Stress and Relaxation

We will use a little visualisation, or creative imagining, now. This will help to consolidate what you have read here, opening you more to the ideas, helping you to develop your unstressing technique further and opening the door in your mind wider to greater creativity and better memory.

Unstressing Yourself 2
Key Exercise: Rhythmic Breathing and Imagination

1. As in earlier exercises, sit quietly, away from all distractions. Turn off your mobile telephone. Light your candle if it is to hand, and it is safe to do so, and loosen any tight clothing. Your candlelight alone will have a calming effect upon you. Place in your mental suitcase any thoughts or ideas you wish to let go.

2. Close your eyes and develop slow, rhythmic breathing as you did earlier. When you have practised this a few times, it will become easier and easier for you. Remember to keep your attention on your abdomen and your solar plexus, as you gradually slow your breathing down to an even, deep rhythm. Always breathe through your nose. Be comfortable. Never force anything to happen. It will always come to you eventually if you are patient and persistent. Use a *gentle firmness* as you practise these techniques.

3. When you feel your breathing has settled down and it is flowing in and out of your body gently and freely, you can begin to use your imagination. To do this, lift your attention slowly upwards, away from your solar plexus, rising, rising until your attention is focused inside your head, where pictures form in your mind. This is the

space which is level with your forehead or brow, at the front, and the crown of your head above it.

4. Wait until you are sure you have found this space. Then you can switch on your imagination.
5. Imagine that just above your head there is a beautiful, warm light. This can be a simple colour that you find appropriate or, alternatively, you can imagine the sun shining just above you.
6. Allow this light to enter your body. Make a picture of this in your mind and imagine the colour flowing downward through your body, filling you with a beautiful wave of calmness as it flows gently downwards.
7. This light fills your head, your neck, your shoulders and arms. It fills your chest and stomach area, your abdomen and your legs and feet. Encourage this light to fill you with its gentle calming influence. Be patient. It will happen.
8. Repeat this image several times, until you feel that every part of you has been touched by the light you have imagined, and can benefit from its calming influence.
9. When you feel that your body is filled with this light and that you can sense a deeper calmness, you can take the relaxation a little further.

Testing How You Are Doing

For a simple test to see how you are doing with this technique, focus on the palms of your hands. The more relaxed you are, the warmer your hands will feel. Focus on them for a few moments. As you practise you will begin to notice the difference. However cold your hands are to begin with, the more you relax, the more your hands will feel

Stress and Relaxation

warm, even slightly tingly, as the blood flow through you increases. A relaxed body has a better and more useful blood flow and therefore a stronger immune system. You will become healthier at all levels.

10. To take this exercise a little further, imagine your body to be so full of calming energy and colour that you become like a light bulb, with light and energy radiating from you in all directions. You literally 'light up' in a very beautiful way.

11. To draw this exercise to a close, take your attention down to your solar plexus and abdomen. Your breath will probably have changed a little; maybe it will have become a little shallower again. Simply switch on your rhythmic breathing, in and out very slowly, as before. Then ground yourself by gradually bringing your attention to your feet on the floor. Finally, open your eyes very slowly, easing yourself back into a normal, awakened state before going about your next activity. Remember to always come out of these exercises gradually and slowly. You will benefit more from them if you do so.

The first time you do this, draw a simple picture, a diagram or cartoon. Introduce a little humour if you like, as it will help you to remember what you have done, and your mind responds more quickly and more profoundly to images and pictures. Oh, and don't forget to extinguish your candle if you have used one!

If you are tired when you do this exercise, you may find, especially in the early days, that you become drowsy and even fall asleep for a few minutes. That is a good thing. If you are tired, it is a signal you shouldn't ignore, and maybe you need more sleep. A catnap can also be a useful way to re-charge the batteries.

In time, this will happen less and less and the process will invigorate you and make you feel more powerful, more energetic and clearer in your head. You can always practise this with a friend, taking turns to lead the other through the stages of the technique. Teaching something to someone else is one of the best ways to learn something ourselves.

Make Your Own Cassette Recording

You can also practise it on your parent, or brother or sister, even a stressed teacher perhaps! Make sure they go through all the stages. If you find it useful, you can also record the stages on a cassette tape. Make a few test levels first of all to ensure you will hear it properly and then record the stages, speaking slowly and clearly, and leaving a pause between each idea and stage of the exercise.

Working with Friends

If you are in school or college, it would be a great idea to practise this with a few good friends or colleagues. Again, you can take turns in leading the session, guiding everyone through the various stages, or you can make a recording so that you all listen to it together. When you lead a session for a small group, you don't entirely miss out in any way as you speak the words. Your subconscious is listening and you will benefit a little also from what you are doing. Your ever-attentive subconscious mind is hearing everything and will try to implement the benefits for you also. And teaching something is always a good way to learn it. Group practice and relaxation sessions are useful, although they should complement your own individual practice. Do both if you can, maybe a group session or one with your friends once a week, but do your own session daily. That is most important.

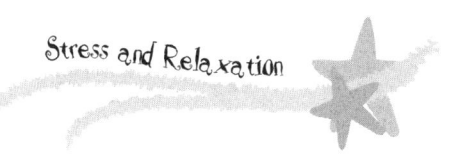

Music and Sounds

Sometimes when practising these exercises, people like to use music. That is fine and can be valuable. We have to be wise in the choice of music. Loud, powerful, quick music is a stimulus and whilst it is great and ideal for dancing, for parties and at other times, it is not generally useful for this type of exercise. It will tend to detract from what you are trying to do and keep bringing your attention back to the present moment too sharply. However, research has shown that, from a creative point of view, some types of music are good for mental exercise. They stimulate the right hemisphere of the brain, helping us to remember things and calming us down.

We all know how healing music can be, as it touches our feelings and emotions in so many ways. For unstressing and relaxation exercises, the best type of music to use is gentle quiet music that naturally makes us slow down, music that doesn't demand our attention too much. Some light, classical music like Debussy, for example, may be suitable, although our individual tastes and preferences also come into play. If we don't like the sounds of violins, for example, then there is no point in listening to it, however beautiful the music may be. The dislike will produce tensions, the very thing you will be seeking to release.

Use your own judgement. If a piece of music helps to create a gentle ambiance that you like, then play it whilst you practise your exercises. You will soon determine whether or not it is distracting or helping you.

Staying Cool

A young sixth form boy in one school I visited told me he found the reggae music of UB40 satisfactory. I was surprised, much as I like UB40, but if it works for him, then I respect his judgement.

I find that as people practise and develop these exercises, they require music less and less, if at all, and find the quiet and stillness most beneficial on its own.

Many people find ambience cassettes or CDs very useful. These generally have natural sounds on them such as birdsong, running water, the waves of the sea and so on and are quite widely available these days. It may be worth trying one of these, especially when starting off with the main Key Exercises.

Cool, Calm, and Chill Out

You will become 'cooler' in your mind as you practise, calmer and more able to be as 'chilled out' as you need to be, whatever is going on around you. Staying cool doesn't mean being almost horizontal like a 1960s hippy. It means being in control so that you can be calm, effective and gently powerful as and when you need to be.

However, a good, simple idea to practise as you progress is that of staying cool. You may be pretty relaxed already, and you will certainly develop a natural, calm response automatically as you develop your techniques. You will become increasingly unshakable, and happier.

Whilst such things may not always seem to work, certainly not on their own, the use of an idea, consistently placed in the mind, can help us to modify and change our behaviour. Sadly, we are often criticised, sometimes unfairly, and told what we cannot do rather than what we can do and achieve. Negative programming is all around us. I was often told I was a 'naughty boy' simply because I was lively and humorous at school. I wasn't perfect but I was basically good. Nonetheless, continual criticism led to me believing myself to be 'You naughty little boy' and I believed 'No, you can't do that!' about many things. We will look at affirmations or affirmative ideas a little later on, but for now, I suggest you use one as a kind of support to the calmness that will naturally unfold from the exercises you are practising.

A Staying Cool Technique

1. Find a small piece of card, like a post card, or a piece of fairly firm paper, something you can slip into your pocket if necessary.
2. On your card, write one of the following:
   'I'm staying cool'
   or
   'I'm staying calm'
   or simply
   'I'm calm'
   Write in large, clear, capital letters so that it is easy to see and read.
3. If you feel inclined, decorate the card and the letters in any way you choose. You can use a few clear, bright colours and enjoy doing it. Treat it as a bit of fun. The idea is serious but you can enjoy it. Make sure, however, that the words are clearly decipherable and readable.
4. When you have prepared your card, read it slowly a few times, then close your eyes and imagine it on your picture screen, inside your head. See it as vividly as you can.

5. Keep the card with you if you can and at odd moments during the day, after taking your pause and relaxation exercises, read it to yourself, either out loud, or inside your head or both.
6. Also, do the same in your journal or notebook. Use the same phrase in both, and use a phrase which really for you does sum up the idea of calming down, and staying cool, calm and collected in every situation.

Drugs, Alcohol and other Things

This portion isn't a nagging sequence for all those who smoke occasionally, have tried and enjoyed an alcoholic drink and may have used or experimented with drugs, both prescribed and unprescribed. I know my own children have done some of the above, and in both my teaching days and some of my therapeutic work, I have met and assisted young people having difficulties stemming from the use and over-use of them all.

The purpose of this book is to help you to realise your potential and develop skills and gifts you undoubtedly have so that you can be happy calm and enjoy the life you have to lead, as much as you possibly can.

However, it is important to understand that all drugs can harm us, and certainly limit us. Of course, when we are taking those things that are medically prescribed for us under the supervision of a doctor or a qualified health professional, we should heed the advice we are given, and be grateful for the help such medication can give when we are unwell. But excessive use of alcohol and the smoking of

Stress and Relaxation

tobacco can and most likely will harm us, and without doubt take away our power to be 'cool' and in control of our lives.

Recently, a friend of mine, Dr Martin Plant, was on British television demonstrating the effects of alcohol upon behaviour. Martin is an expert and leading researcher into the uses and abuses of alcohol, having published many papers and reports on the subject, and currently lecturing with his wife, Moira, at the University of Western England at Bristol. For the test, an experienced stunt driver was chosen to perform certain set manoeuvres in a car and he executed them perfectly at the first attempt. He was then given a small amount of alcohol and asked to repeat the manoeuvres. This time he made a few small mistakes, nothing major, but small errors nonetheless. After another drink, his driving deteriorated badly and after further alcohol, his driving became very dangerous and reckless. Yet, this experienced, clever driver, when interviewed, actually thought he was still driving well, even when intoxicated with alcohol. He wasn't aware that the alcohol was taking his power away from him, and that he was losing control. He was becoming less and less effective.

Alcohol is a drug, in fact it is a poison, and all drugs can delude us, especially those that are particularly psycho-active and are designed primarily to influence how we think and feel. The temporary euphoria such things bring is always followed by a similar downward movement. Most of us know what a hangover is like after a wild, boozy party. And science has shown us the polluted lungs and damaged hearts that consistent heavy smoking brings.

You have a choice. You can stay cool, creative and in control and these exercises will help you to do that. And if you already a drinker, smoker or drug user, and feel it is out of control, you should first seek professional help. But these exercises will help to reduce addiction and create a space in your mind and your life where you can exercise real choice and take control.

The choice is yours. You have a great potential, whoever you are. Don't give your power away.

Summary of Activities

- *Mind over Matter*

Try the mind over matter exercises. They will demonstrate how what we think and feel affects our bodies.

- *Unstressing Yourself 1*

Learn to loosen the tensions in your neck and shoulders. These are major points of accumulated physical stress.

- *Key Exercise: Unstressing Yourself – Breathing*

Once a day practise establishing an even, slow rhythm in your breathing, calming and slowing down everything in you for a while.

- *The Duvet Technique*

See how well you are progressing with your deep, rhythmic breathing, by practising for a few minutes in bed, before you go to sleep. Watch the duvet!

- *Unstressing Yourself 2*

Key Exercise: Rhythmic Breathing and Imagination

Use your imagination with your breathing to fill your body with energy, from your head to your toes, and imagine it radiating into your space around you. Consider making a simple recording of this for your own use and maybe working with friends.

- *A Staying Cool Technique*

Use your postcard memo to affirm 'I am staying cool. I am calm'.

Chapter 3
Exams, Tests and Interviews

Most of us become a little nervous when we have to face a test or examination, or need to attend some kind of interview. Of course, there seem to be those who either have nerves made of steel or simply don't care (at least, that's what they may say) but I was always quite anxious, no matter how many tests or assessments I did.

We tend to have the same experience when we have to give a performance. As a singer, both with a rock band and in other music, I was always a little anxious before a performance, even though I could sing well and enjoyed it enormously once the initial 'butterflies' were overcome and the show commenced. It can be argued that, to some extent, this is a natural and perhaps useful experience, at least to some degree, as it prevents us from being too complacent and casual, and keeps us alert and on our toes.

The Fight or Flight Response

However, this mechanism, sometimes called 'fight or flight response', can become a nuisance. Whilst it can give us a valuable signal that we may need to be concentrated on the task in hand, it can also go into overdrive and make us unnecessarily anxious, leading to a less than satisfactory performance in whatever situation we find ourselves.

The 'fight or flight' response is in your solar plexus. It is a mechanism that is supposed to protect you, to warn you there is a difficulty by pumping extra adrenaline from your adrenal glands to increase heart rate and metabolism, so that you can either stay and 'fight' whatever is threatening you, or use the extra power and energy to take 'flight' and run away to safety.

This was all very well when, as primitive beings, we needed to fight our enemies or the savage beasts that tended to attack our homes, or if it looked hopeless, enabled us to run away quickly, so we could find safety somewhere. The problem we have is that this mechanism still works in us when we can actually do neither. Instead of fighting with our enemy or escaping and running away to safety, in many situations we have to stay and go through whatever is making us anxious. We have to 'tough it out'.

Without some strategy to dilute and manage the response, this can be a difficult and even painful process. The tension in the stomach can also make us sick with fear and, because the solar plexus is located near the stomach, it can put us off our food in a big way, eventually leading to eating problems and digestive disorders.

We have to learn how to channel this 'nervous' energy, to ride on the butterflies, 'the fright', and convert them into something more useful and more creative.

The pattern of exercises in this book will help you to gradually reduce your general level of anxiety and provide you with a growing, deep-seated sense of calmness. In addition to this, there are various techniques you can employ to clear fears and anxieties, both specific problems and those that seem to be less defined.

Energy Centres

Energy centres, also referred to in acupuncture, shiatsu massage, and many of the natural healing traditions, are invisible to the naked eye, but exist in what is known as the subtle energy field of human beings.

Scientists and medical professionals in the West are now increasingly accepting the existence of these energy fields and centres, and both technical as well as intuitive methods of locating them have been and are being developed. One

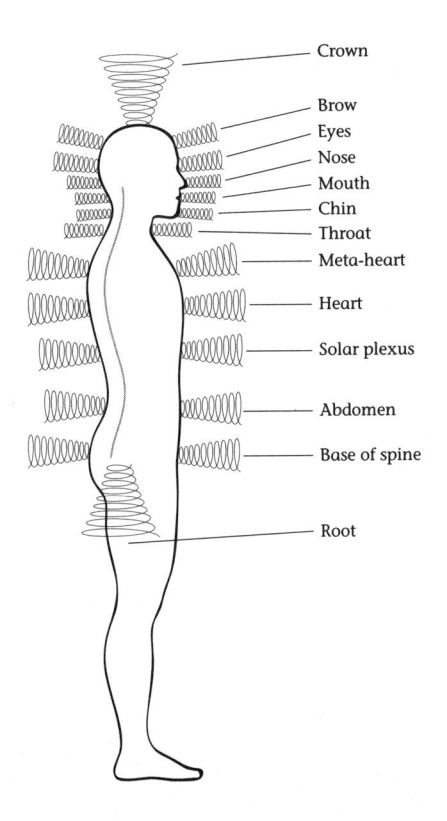

- Crown
- Brow
- Eyes
- Nose
- Mouth
- Chin
- Throat
- Meta-heart
- Heart
- Solar plexus
- Abdomen
- Base of spine
- Root

famous method is that of Kirlian photography, developed by the Russian scientist Semyon Kirlian in 1939. He discovered a method of photographing an electrical field existing around the human hand and body, and then around all living things, including plants, leaves and flowers.

We considered the solar plexus earlier, but there are other very important centres that I will mention to you. Experts disagree on exactly how many there are altogether, but for our purposes, we will look at a few significant ones located parallel to the spine.

Important to us in this book are the Heart Centre, the Brow Centre in the forehead (often referred to as the third eye because it is where our imagination 'sees') and the Root Centre at the base of the spine. There are others, but these are the ones we need to understand a little for our purposes. A diagram of the 13 major centres is shown on the opposite page.

The Heart Centre

The location of the heart is easy to find. It is a space close to the centre of the chest. A good way to locate it is simply to think of someone you love, or a place you love deeply,

Linking heart to heart.

like an old friend or member of your family, or a place you love to visit on holiday. If you imagine it powerfully, it will generate a quite remarkable and beautiful sensation, above your solar plexus somewhere in the centre of your chest. Practise it and you will feel it. That is your heart centre. It is the place to where people that we love or want to protect are attracted.

The Brow Centre

The brow centre is also easy to locate. Every time you have used your imagination in this book, to create a picture of an image inside your head, it has formed just inside your forehead, or brow. This is where the brow energy centre is located. Even if you do not form pictures easily in your imagination, and some of us don't, none the less, any thought you have will stimulate this area. We tend to think inside our heads.

The Root Centre

This space is located at the bottom of your spine. It is a little more difficult to 'feel' or sense. It is very active when we hear strong music with a distinctive rhythm. Such a regular beat in music stimulates us in this area and it can be difficult to stop our feet tapping and our body swaying.

We can also feel the effects of this centre when we are agitated, angry or extremely excited, as ripples run up our spine, like an electrical force. Elton John in one of his songs uses the words 'reality runs up my spine'. That feeling is also an indication of energy from this area being stimulated in you, tingling up your spinal column. Test this by playing some popular dance music, and then try to keep your feet still and stop your body from swaying. It will be difficult.

Exams, Tests and Interviews

Clearing Fear from the Solar Plexus

1. Sit quietly, taking a pause for a few moments. Focus upon your breathing, bringing your attention to your solar plexus as you do so. Feel the breath as it flows in and out of your body, establishing the slow, gentle rhythm you have been practising.
2. When you feel quite calm, call into your mind a specific fear or anxiety you have, one that perhaps has been troubling you for some time, an idea that gives you butterflies. Whatever it is, you have no need to fear it. You can change your attitude to it and the way you think and feel about it. Try to be aware of how you feel in your solar plexus when you call the idea into your mind.
3. Imagine this fear to be a dirty, muddy colour, caught in your solar plexus like a ball of unpleasant energy you would rather not keep with you.
4. Next, imagine this ball of energy rising slowly upwards from your solar plexus towards your heart energy centre, in the centre of your chest.
5. As this energy moves, it begins to change colour, becoming clearer, less muddy and dirty, gradually changing to a clear, bright ball of energy next to your heart. This can be any bright colour you like, although a deep rose pink is a good one to imagine. In your mind, imagine the fear leaving you, floating away from you, like a bubble. If you have been afraid to do something, say to yourself, out loud if you can, 'I can do it now, I can …' whatever it is you wish to do or have been afraid to attempt.
6. Then imagine a wave of energy from your solar plexus pouring downwards, through your legs and feet into the ground. You will feel more confident now.

7. The feelings of fear and anxiety will diminish and ultimately, with a little practice, will dissolve and dissipate completely.

You will begin to release the fear and the tension around it, so that you can take any action necessary to deal with it or the situation. If it is a deep-seated fear, you may be surprised how your attitudes change. Say to yourself, 'I'm free of this fear now.'

One young boy of twelve came to see me with his mother. He was afraid of going to school and had experienced several problems including a little bullying in the past. The bullying had been dealt with, but the fear remained as a bad memory he couldn't shake off, and he was afraid to go to school. The boy had seen several psychologists but the fear remained. We used this exercise a few times and he was able to face his fear, go to school in a more comfortable frame of mind and he is currently doing well.

Fear of an Individual

Sometimes, we fear a particular individual. We may have good reason for this and we should always discuss such problems with our parents, friends, teachers, those who can help us take the most appropriate action. Never hide such a fear or suppress it, especially if you fear harm to yourself.

But it may be that there is someone we find difficult, who seems a little unkind or difficult to get along with. I remember a much bigger boy at school when I was about ten years old. He was verbally very aggressive and rude and often tried to make fun of me. If you have such an experience with someone, where the fear is a mental or emotional one, use this last exercise with that person in mind. This time you focus on the person in your solar plexus and then gradually lift the thought slowly upwards into your heart as the colour changes.

You will feel the difference even after the first time you do it, and you will notice eventually that, as the tension and fear in you decreases, the attitude of the other person towards you may also improve. He or she will probably leave you alone and may even become pleasant and affable towards you. Things will certainly improve.

I also used this approach with a lecturer at a local college who came to see me because she was having problems with a rather aggressive colleague. She practised the exercise very diligently, over a period of some weeks, and the situation improved considerably, so much so, that she expressed her surprise at how much improved their relationship had become.

Again, this exercise does not replace seeking help and advice where you think you are very threatened, or being treated in a cruel and unfair way. *Always* tell others who can help you with your problem or concerns and take sensible action where it is clear you need to do so. Some persistent fears may call for some counselling. But this exercise will help enormously with those difficult relationships that cause anxiety and tension, impeding your ability to be calm and happy.

This is an excellent way to stay cool.

The Ten Finger Technique

Sometimes, we need something simple to slow us down and calm us down. I first developed this technique when I was

Staying Cool

young. In a tense situation, or when you feel a wave of anxiety, perhaps before an exam or test, you can use this quickly and simply. Practise it a few times beforehand, until you can do it easily. Then you can use it at any time to clear the butterflies.

1. Starting with your right hand, gently press the top of your first or index finger against your thumb, for a couple of seconds, and then release it slowly, rotating your thumb a few times gently across the surface of your fingertip in a clockwise direction. As you do this, simply think the words 'Release and Calm'.
2. Move your thumb to the next finger on your right hand and repeat the exercise, gently pressing and releasing with your thumb and then gently rotating your thumb a few times around the surface, slowly thinking 'Release and Calm'.
3. Do this with each of your fingers on your right hand and then return to your thumb and index finger where you started. This time, gently press your thumb with your index finger, release and make a few clockwise rotations with it as you repeat 'Release and Calm'.
4. Move to your left hand and go through the same process, commencing and finishing with your thumb and index finger.

At first, you may well feel a little strange practising this, but it will work for you once you have it clearly in your mind. You can add to its effectiveness by taking a slow breath in and out, as you press and then release your finger and thumb at each point. This isn't essential, but it is useful. I have taught this to many young people and you can use this technique, fairly quickly and simply, in any situation. It will help you to release whatever feeling you wish to release and be calmer and more focused. It is simple, but very effective. Try it!

Memory

The worst advice we can ever give anyone is 'Forgive and forget', but people often say it. Forgive we can. Forget we cannot, at least not permanently. There are those who never forget anything. They seem to have a 'photographic memory', and appear to have no problem reading a page of a book and then recalling it in almost perfect detail. Such individuals appear to have a natural ability to recall everything they have either read or observed with remarkable clarity and in the most enticing detail.

There are two main strands of memory:
- *Short-term* memory deals with more immediate issues, for example where you just put your cup of coffee, your spectacles and so on.
- *Long-term* memory stores facts and information for later reference, such as where you were on holiday last year, the trips you made and so on. It also deals with how to do things, usually instinctively.

Of course, these two overlap and short-term, apparently less significant things do find their way into the mental filing cabinet, sometimes cluttering the access you need to the important information and ideas. The memory drawer gets a bit full!

The unstressing techniques in this book will help you to clear the unnecessary details you no longer need to store. Your mind will filter them out as you relax. In the early

Staying Cool

stages of learning unstressing and relaxation techniques, many irritating, often trivial thoughts even from way back in the past will seek to grab your attention and pull your concentration away from the exercise you are doing.

However, unstressing and using your old mental suitcase will help to file them away separately, so they don't block the road to important ideas and thoughts you store for later reference. But again, we never forget anything.

My oldest son has always been very useful as a co-navigator on a journey in the car. As a small boy, not only would he remember the way home better than anyone else, but if we had to make a return trip, he would remember the route and especially the key important landmarks better than anyone else. 'We turned left at that funny tree!' he would shout, as I fumbled around, trying to recall where to go next, looking for a familiar sight from a previous visit.

One reason for this was that he was visually very alert. He allowed pictures and images to register clearly in his mind and he could call upon them with ease, so long as he was interested and wanted to do so. Like all of us, he could be a little selective, and conveniently 'forget' those things that didn't seem so important or urgent to him!

Our brain cells process our thoughts and they are able to tap into our memory and bring to the surface the thoughts and ideas we have tucked away in our mental filing cabinet, deep in our minds. Whatever our mind is, it is not our brain. Our mind exists in a kind of energy field that the brain can dip into, as it needs to.

The work of such eminent scientists, psychologists and researchers as C.J. Jung, Abraham Maslow and Dr Rupert Sheldrake, have supported the idea that the brain accesses the field of the mind, rather than actually being the mind.

I have worked with a number of people who have suffered brain cell damage, either from disease such as Alzheimer's, following a stroke or cerebral haemorrhage, or an accident of some kind. In many cases, memory has become impaired and thoughts from the past seem to be lost, only to be regained later on, even though the brain cells normally considered to be performing that function have been damaged beyond repair. This is because the brain learns how to use other cells to access the mind and the memories and thoughts contained within it. If this were not true, then no such improvements would be possible.

Different parts of the brain are used to process different aspects of our function. The two hemispheres mentioned earlier are together known as the cerebral cortex. This is generally recognised as the area of the brain that manages our most sophisticated functions, including our ability to learn from what we experience around us in our everyday lives and the memory we store of those experiences through our senses.

The left hemisphere of this cortex helps us to speak, use language, write and process intellectual ideas. The right side or hemisphere is connected with our creative nature, our appreciation of form, colour, feeling and so on. Since our memories include all of these phenomena – we picture and feel as well as record and analyse our experiences – then we need to ensure we use our whole brain and both hemispheres of the cerebral cortex to access our vast memory.

It is perhaps a good idea to pause here and reinforce these ideas.

> - **You have a vast and remarkable mind. You record and place everything in your memory, in your mental filing cabinet.**
> - **You can recall everything you have ever read, seen and experienced.**
> - **You forget nothing. You remember everything.**

Close your eyes and use your imagination for a few moments. I have used this type of exercise with young and old clients and it has proved most beneficial.

Key Exercise: Linking Brain Hemispheres

1. Imagine there is a wonderful, marvelous machine inside your head. You call it your brain and you can imagine it however you choose. It is a wonderful piece of equipment.
2. At the top of this machine are the two hemispheres of the brain, one on the left and one on the right. Imagine them as two coloured areas, perhaps the left-hand side as yellow and the right-hand side as blue.
3. Imagine a corridor linking the two halves of your brain; it connects the left to the right, the logical to the imaginative part.
4. As this link forms, so the colours begin to mix and the yellow colour flows from the left-hand side to the right-hand side and the blue flows from the right to the left, producing a bright beautiful mixed green colour throughout the whole brain as the two halves link and work more closely together.

When you have done this, open your eyes slowly and then draw a picture of what you have done. Keep the picture simple. Make it like a sketch or cartoon, and colour it in, perhaps doing a 'before' and 'after' drawing. This will reinforce the idea and make it more powerful and effective, and the act of planning the drawing (left brain), executing it (right brain), links the two halves most effectively. This linking of the two hemispheres of the brain makes us more balanced and mentally more efficient.

Another simple activity you can try for this purpose is as follows:
1. Close your eyes and place your attention inside your head, where the pictures form in your imagination.
2. Imagine that in front of you there is a large tennis court, with a net across the middle and a player at each end.
3. The player on the right hits a large tennis ball across the net to the player at the other end, who then returns the ball back from the left to the right.
4. Watch the ball travel from right to left, and back again several times, and imagine the ball to be travelling slowly, slow enough for you to follow it in your mind.

When you have finished, bring your focus gradually back into the room and open your eyes slowly.

Key Exercise: Accessing Memory

You are going to develop this idea a little further, so that you can balance your mind and open the channels to your memory. If you already have an excellent recall of facts and information as you need them, then this is perhaps one Key

Staying Cool

Exercise that you could omit from your practice. However, I suggest you try it at least a few times as it can only help things to improve and certainly won't impede what you have already done.

1. Take a pause and close your eyes.
2. Relax by focusing upon your solar plexus for a few moments and slowing your breath until it is even and rhythmic. You should be quite able to do this by now.
3. Bring your attention up to your head, and think of the two areas of your brain, left and right. Think of them linking as before so that the left and right merge to form one single unit.
4. When you have imagined this, be aware that above your head there is a large funnel through which thoughts and ideas pour into your brain as and when you may need them.
5. As these thoughts, like little bubbles, pop into your head, your brain files them away so that you can access them whenever you choose to. Remember that inside your mind there is a huge filing cabinet, just like you saw in Chapter 1.
6. Picture that filing cabinet now and see all the drawers in it. It has thousands and thousands of drawers.
7. Think of a title or simple heading now, perhaps 'My Family' or 'My School'. Look for the drawer in your filing cabinet with 'My Family' or 'My School' on it.
8. Open the drawer, and inside is all the information you need on the subject: pictures of everyone's faces, the clothes they wear, perhaps other details written on sheets of paper, such as birth dates, favourite food, and so on. Every detail you have ever known about your family or friends is here.

9. You can explore inside the file if you wish and select the one you want. Just place the word in your mind: 'Mum', or 'John', or whatever title you give them, and there is a file especially for them with everything about them on it and everything you have ever shared together.
10. Remember what you see on the file and then put it back in its drawer, close the filing cabinet and imagine stepping back from it.
11. Gradually focus on your solar plexus and your breathing for a few moments. Ground yourself and open your eyes.
12. Now write down on a piece of paper as much as you can remember about the person whose file you took out for a while. Simply write, and the information will begin to flow.

Your thoughts string together like flags on a string.

You will remember things that you thought you had long forgotten. And the more you try this exercise, the more you will remember each time you visit your inner filing cabinet. With sufficient practice, all you will need to do is pause, think of your filing system and call up the file and it will give to you the appropriate stream of thought you need to remember.

Thoughts String Together

It is useful to be aware that your thoughts string together, rather like flags on a string. As you pull out one idea or one particular thought, it will bring with it another, connected to it. By developing your filing system, you will be able to link the thoughts together in the most appropriate sequence, so that you can work creatively and also in a structured, ordered fashion, one idea or memory leading to the next most appropriate one, and so on. If you tell your mind what you want and you are consistent, it will give to you what you need, as you need it.

Filing things Away: Mnemonics

A mnemonic is a tool that helps us to identify something and call it to mind as we need it.

When we are very young, we especially use smell, taste and touch, all very physical ways of experiencing our world. You can probably recall some of the smells from the kitchen when you were small, when someone was cooking. Maybe you can recall the smell of your mother's linen, the aroma of your parents' clothes, or the perfume from the flowers that grew in your garden as a child. Then there is also the smell of crayons, a new box of Plasticine, or a new toy.

You will certainly recall the tastes of the food of your childhood, the sweet, the bitter, the hot and spicy and the bland. Pause for a moment to do that. Take your mind back to when you were a small child, thinking particularly of the tastes and aromas from those days. You may be surprised at what you remember!

Also linked with this part of your memory is touch, the way you feel things, mainly with your hands. You will recall rough things and smooth things, soft things and hard ones. Textures often fascinate us when we are small children.

We learn and store information through our physical memories, what we learn, when we do something: *smell, taste* and *touch*.

We also learn by hearing. Much teaching in college and schools is auditory. How often does a teacher cry out to the class, 'Come on, listen please!' We are encouraged to absorb by hearing, and you as a student will be expected to learn much by this method, and store the ideas and information you hear, deep in your memory.

Increasingly, we learn things visually. We use television, often in preference to radio, where we both see and hear, and where the dominance is visual. An interesting way to compare the two is to listen to the radio commentary of a sports event, for example a football or cricket match, or a race of some kind that is also being shown simultaneously on the television. First of all, try to listen to the radio commentary, and watch the TV picture at the same time, with the volume turned down on your TV set. Then turn down the radio and turn up the TV commentary and you should notice a considerable difference.

The solely auditory (radio) commentary has to give you a lot of information. It has to help you create a picture in your mind of the event that is as clear and complete as it can be, as if you were there in the stadium. On the TV it is different. You can see what is happening so the commentator doesn't have to describe the action. The commentary is less intense, less detailed and often less direct, complementing the pictures rather than building them.

For example:
- *Radio Commentary*: 'Johnson now has the ball, running down the right-hand side of the pitch, but still in his own half, the opposing defenders closing in on him ...'
- *TV Commentary*: 'Johnson, showing us his pace ...'

Visual learning is becoming more widely appreciated now and it is a very natural way for us to place things in our minds. Most of us learn better from a story, full of images, than from a pile of facts contained in words and figures.

We are very visual. Our minds work with images, colours and symbols. Yet this is often neglected in our learning programmes. When you read this text, you may initially 'hear' the words in your head, but then (hopefully) you will form images to go with them.

Most of us assimilate information and instructions much more quickly and effectively when they are accompanied by pictures, such as in a sound system manual, car handbook or DIY instructions.

To learn and to have an effective memory system in which everything is stored and labelled clearly you need to use good mnemonics or memory tools and ensure you have stored things well in your mental filing cabinet.

Exams, Tests and Interviews

Music and Words – Whole Brain Learning

This activity helps you to use your whole brain, both hemispheres, together. It is called 'whole brain' learning. When you sing a song, the whole brain is involved. Your left hemisphere processes the words and the right hemisphere connects with the music. Hence you can learn words much more quickly and permanently if you either sing them or use appropriate music to stimulate the right brain as you read and consider words, facts and figures.

1. Take a couple of lines from the text of a book, perhaps one you are using for study. It can be any book, so long as you can read the text out loud.
2. Also, find a piece of music, preferably something light and tuneful, even a nursery rhyme tune. Something light and simple.
3. Play the music and read the text slowly, out loud to yourself. Read it as clearly as you can.
4. Then begin to sing it to the tune, several times over. It is useful if it is a tune you know and like. Do enjoy it and laugh if you wish to as you do it. The pleasure of laughter helps us to remember things. We tend to reminisce happy memories easier than anything else.
5. Close the book, maybe listening to the tune a while longer and then briefly forget the whole process for the moment.
6. A day or so later, sit down and recall the tune. As you do so, some of the words of the text will come back into your mind. Eventually, all of it will. You may even see the page before you in your mind.

Some of us prefer to learn through left-brain, logical, analytical ways. Some of us prefer pictures and images. To retain things you need to have both facilities active.

Staying Cool

Colour, Sound and Revision

One of the simplest mnemonics is colour. Most of us like colour, and by colouring or using colour in and around text we have to read and learn, or the summary notes we have made from it, we give ourselves a simple, powerful aid to remembering.

Again, you never forget anything. Everything you experience goes into your mind and can be retrieved as you wish. But filing it away carefully makes it easier.

Here are some tips on learning and revising:

1. *Sound*

If possible, as you read through some text that you need to study and learn, play some gentle music. It has been shown that light, classical music, like Vivaldi's 'Four Seasons' or Bach's 'Brandenburg Concertos', is especially useful. If you don't really like that kind of music, try something else that you can listen to, gentle music that will not draw your attention away from the words or the text you are studying. Also, ensure there are no words to this music, simply flowing sounds. The secret is to use music with a regular beat or rhythm; around 60 beats per minute is ideal but not essential. This practice alone will help you to remember things and take them deeper inside your memory, keeping them available until you need them.

2. *Revision Notes*

Make your notes from your text, for later revision, choosing the headings as you find them useful. If you have read through using the method described in (1), you will find it easier to summarise the text and the important points will leap out into your mind more easily as your read through again. As you make your notes, play your music quietly in the background and you may also find it useful to read out aloud the important pieces as you write them down.

3. Colour

When you have reached a convenient point of note making, perhaps no more than a side of paper, pause for a moment. Read through the text of your notes, altering them until you are happy with them. Then find some coloured pencils or pens and either put a coloured border around each headed section, idea, or topic, or colour lightly under the words, especially those that are most important to recall. If you have coloured writing pens, you can also change colour as you write, changing colours for each idea or topic or as you write down each new chunk of information. Avoid making it too complicated, but do make it bright and interesting.

4. Symbols

We love symbols. Our mind works in symbols, which are pictographs, a little like the words in oriental pictographic languages such as Chinese. Symbols are immediate memory aides or mnemonics. Our road traffic signs are symbolic, visual summaries that we can recognise immediately and know what they are telling us. You may like to add a symbol occasionally near the text. It can be a simple, cartoon-like form, nothing too elaborate, preferably linked to the text. For example, if you are learning about botany, draw a simple tree and colour it green. Or maybe you are reading and learning about the reign of a King, and the dates he was on the throne. Draw a simple crown and write his name and dates upon it. Say it as you do so, listening to your music, and it will flow into your mind.

Revision Strategies

Short, crisp periods of revision for reconnecting and familiarising with topics needed for tests or exams, are best.

After a short period, perhaps twenty minutes or so, it is useful to take a break for a while and then return to your studies. Once half an hour or so has gone, your attention and concentration will decline if you don't break.

Before any period of revision, take a pause for a few moments and put any thoughts you don't need just now in your mental suitcase. It need only be a brief pause, as you will by now, hopefully, have practised the unstressing techniques sufficiently to link into them fairly easily and quickly. This will also aid your memory access and increase your concentration span, that is the length of time you can concentrate effectively on your work or text. Whatever you do, take regular short breaks, have a drink, maybe a little stroll or walk and then return.

Try not to revise when you are tired. It is counter-productive and it is better left until you are more alert, more awake. The early hours of the morning, between 5.00 and 7.00am, are far better than those just before midnight.

Before you start your revision, say to yourself, 'I will remember this clearly.' When you have completed it, take it into your inner filing cabinet.

1. Take a brief pause.
2. Remember how the two hemispheres of your brain are linked together, perfectly.
3. Imagine your inner filing cabinet as clearly as you can. See its many drawers.

4. Open a drawer and imagine that you place inside it, one by one, the notes you have been revising, seeing the colours on the page as you do so around the words, and also any image or symbol on the page. Think of the music that you were listening to as you read through it all.
5. Again, think the words 'I will remember this clearly as and when I need to.' Then write the headings or subject matter on the label on the front of the drawer in colours, adding a symbol if you wish. Think 'I am filing you away in my mind carefully.'
6. Close the drawer, and gradually bring your filing session to a close.

The whole filing session need only take a few moments. And you can adapt the above process to suit your own needs as your experience will dictate and show you.

However, do use the *music*, add some *colour* to your notes, and *say out loud* the key words, ideas or things you need to remember most. These key ideas, when remembered, will help you to remember a core idea in a subject, and will then lead you from one thought to another, as you recall all the information associated with it, that you need to know and utilise at that moment.

Your filing system is intelligent and will give you what you need, as you need it. Trust it. It will work for you.

Making Notes

A word on structuring notes. There is no panacea here. There are as many ways as there are individuals and you will have a pretty good idea what works best for you. You will soon get to know the key ideas or headings that will lead you through your mental filing system to the information locked up there. Using these methods, your notes will be firmly lodged in your mind and will be much more accessible than before.

Examinations

In an examination or test, it is important to be reasonably relaxed, as you should be if you have practised your unstressing and taken your pauses. It is also important to relax and then to link with the question you are being asked to answer. (See 'Reading the Question'.)

Oral Tests

In an examination, of course, listen carefully. Also you can connect with whoever is speaking to you, asking you a question, in the following way. Practise a few times in 'dummy' situations, with a friend or parent before the real examination, so you can do it quickly.

1. Think of the space around your heart, the place described earlier. This is the point in you where your empathy, your ability to link with others and really have an understanding with them is found.
2. Imagine that you are able to connect this heart energy point in you with that of the examiner or tester through an invisible thread. This link enables you to 'feel' as well as 'hear' the question being asked and will help you to understand quickly and effectively what you need to say in response.
3. When the oral session or examination has finished, pull your 'invisible thread' back into your heart as you leave.

Exams, Tests and Interviews

A young boy I once helped to overcome his exam nerves found this an extremely simple and useful way of being at ease in a number of oral tests he had to undertake. You can do the same and it will work for you.

Key Exercise: Reading the Question

This is very important, especially where you have to choose which questions to answer in an examination, although it applies to all exam situations.

1. When you first gaze at the examination paper, remember that, assuming you have been properly guided and taught by your teachers (and I am sure that you will have been) you know exactly what the examination needs from you. It is all filed away perfectly.
2. Read the questions carefully, slowly, *three* times. If you have to choose a question, then again pause, and use your heart area. It will help you to decide which question to answer. There is a wonderful scanner inside your head. As you scan the questions, they will link via this scanner with your inner filing cabinet.
3. When you know the question you have to respond to, after reading it three times, let your filing cabinet spring into action. It will open the drawers as you need them, and the information will flow through your mind, *as you need it*. Your mind will access, carefully and perfectly, the stream of thoughts and ideas you need so that you can express yourself perfectly within the framework of the question.

My experience, as a former teacher, as a dad, and working with young students, suggests that the reason many students make errors in tests and exams is because

As you scan the questions they will link with your filing cabinet.

they do not read and connect properly with the question they are being asked. The consequence is that the wrong thought train is stimulated and an incorrect or incomplete answer is given.

By reading the question three times, you allow it to truly penetrate through your mind, into your subconscious, bringing its meaning into the vast realm of information in the filing cabinet where all you need is stored.

So remember, *scan and read your question three times*, slowly, and then the information you need will flow to you more easily.

The Interview

You will most probably have to attend many interviews, maybe for college, or a training programme, or perhaps for

Exams, Tests and Interviews

a job. Whatever the situation, there is a new important principle to follow here.

My experience has shown me over the years that there is a right place in life for everyone to go, and for everyone to be. And there is perfect activity for everyone to do. No two of us are the same and this is right and good, and the way it should be.

In an interview, it is important to be relaxed and at ease. Again, the unstressing technique will help this considerably and enable you to feel at ease in most situations. Of course, there are certain obvious things to consider before any interview that you know you are going to attend.

1. Get a good night's sleep the night before so you feel good and energetic that day. The lack of energy that tiredness brings can make you edgy and anxious.
2. Dress comfortably and smartly. You need to be yourself so don't go over the top, but remember, those interviewing you will probably have smartened up a little for the occasion, so it is polite for you to do the same. A simple, tidy appearance can be very striking and get things off to a good start.
3. A practical tip: don't drink lots of coffee before entering the interview room. Coffee is fine in small doses, but the caffeine can over-stimulate the nerves and eventually make you over-active and too hyped up. It is also a diuretic, and may make more visits to the toilet necessary, perhaps when you least wish to! I remember interviewing a candidate for a position in a department I ran, and the poor young lady had drunk so much coffee, prior to the interview, she had to be excused half way through to visit the ladies room!

4. Ongoing practice of the Key Unstressing and Staying Cool exercises will make you calmer anyway, but maybe do a little of your slow, rhythmic breathing and the 'ten finger' technique before you enter the interview.

Being 'You'

For an interview, remember some key ideas.

- *It is important to be you*

People often make the mistake at an interview of trying to impress too much. A good interviewer will often spot this anyway. In any interview, simply be yourself. By being relaxed, those interviewing will get to see the *real* you and you will do yourself justice. A relaxed mind will always bring ideas through, as you need them, from your mental filing cabinet.

It is also important to remember that you wish to be in the right place in life, doing whatever is right and best for you at that time.

Think about that for a moment and read it again. It is important. It is the only way you can be truly happy and fulfilled.

- *There is a right place for you*

There is a college, university, job or whatever it is you are seeking, that is right for you. By being you, relaxed, honest, and cool, you will find the right situation. It may not be at the first attempt. People often find that a job they failed to get would not have been right for them anyway, and something much more suitable came along for them later on. Sometimes that college place isn't the right one; there is something better further on for you.

Remember also, that if you take on a job or course that is not the right one for you, you may be uncomfortable in it and experience many problems. I have seen this happen frequently. It is good to be ambitious, but be ambitious for the situation that is best for you. And why should you try to get a place or position that could be inferior to one that comes along later on!

By being yourself, you will find it and it will find you.

Cool, calm, relaxed people are magnetic; they attract things to themselves.

- *An interview is a 2-way process*

Interviewers may wish to discover things about you, but you also wish to discover things about them. You will usually be asked if you have any questions. It is important to prepare some of your own questions beforehand. Write them down on a small postcard and keep this in your pocket. Of course, some questions will probably surface as a consequence of the interview, but you can be at least partly prepared.

There is a Key Exercise here I suggest you have in your mind.

Key Exercise: Linking with Interviewers

1. Before entering the interview, think of those two energy centres mentioned earlier: one at the solar plexus and one at the heart.
2. If you feel a little nervous, imagine lifting that fear upwards from your solar plexus into your heart. You can do this very quickly and it will calm you.
3. Then remember that those interviewing you want to see the real you, the best in you. They want to understand

you and who you are. To help this process, imagine an invisible link is formed between your heart centre and those heart spaces of the interviewers. Again, just do it briefly, and slowly, and as you do so, smile! You will find this will help you enormously and make you feel 'warm-hearted' to them, as they will to you.

4. At the end of the interview, when you say 'thank you' as you leave, imagine that this link then dissolves.

- *Dummy interview*

Before any interview, try a dummy or practice interview. Your friends, parents or teachers may help you here. Of course, you cannot practise all the questions, but simply going through and acting out the process like a play, will help you, and your mind will recognise the situation when you meet it for real.

Script it out, set out some chairs and just work through an imaginary situation. It doesn't matter if you laugh a little whilst doing it. Enjoy it and it will help you to prepare.

- *Answering questions*

When asked a question, always pause briefly before answering clearly and slowly. This gives your mind time to process the question and link into the correct part of your mental filing system so you can give your best answer. When you know that you *do* know the answer, give yourself time. Don't waffle as that is easily spotted by interviewers. Your mind will give you what you need. Stay cool! Remember these words and the techniques you have at your disposal. Breathe slowly and stay cool!

If you find that you really *don't know* the answer to a

question because the information is outside your experience, be honest. Politely say so:

'I'm sorry I am unable to answer that.'

or

'I have yet to study that area.'

or

'I have no knowledge of that as yet.'

or something similar.

'That's interesting. I didn't know that.'

A good interviewer will appreciate simple honesty much more than a lot of meaningless drivel attempting to conceal a lack of knowledge. But most important of all: be yourself.

> **Think to yourself: 'I'll give of my best here. If it is right for me, then I will get the place (job or whatever). If it isn't, then there is something else for me, elsewhere.' And that is always true.**

Summary of Activities

- *Clearing Fear from the Solar Plexus*

Practise moving fears or anxieties from your solar plexus to your heart space, using colour as you do so. You can do this for both people and situations.

- *The Ten Finger Technique*

Try the Ten Finger Technique and use it as a quick method for slowing yourself and calming yourself down.

Staying Cool

- *Key Exercise: Linking Brain Hemispheres*

This is a very valuable exercise for the development of your memory and unlocking your creativity. Try both exercises and see which one is most comfortable for you.

- *Key Exercise: Accessing Memory*

Balance your mind and open the pathway to your mental filing cabinet where everything you need is stored.

- *Music and Words – Whole Brain Learning*

Experiment using words and music to learn some text you wish to retain.

- *Revision Strategies*

Use music, colour, symbols and speech (sound) to place things firmly into your memory.

- *Examinations*

Key Exercise: Reading the Question

Be calm, stay cool and read the questions three times for clarity. Link with the questions through your heart space so that you can understand what it is asking of you.

- *The Interview*

Key Exercise: Linking with Interviewers

Be you and link with the interviewers so that you do yourself justice. Have an open heart and link with those interviewing you in a friendly, relaxed and open way. You only want the right situation to emerge for you, as there is a place somewhere that is perfect for you.

Chapter 4
Your Imagination

One of the most powerful tools you have to help you shape your life is your imagination. And everyone has an imagination. You will have already explored it a little earlier, testing to see how the pictures you build in your mind affect your body, your strength and how you feel generally.

It is now accepted that the use of the imagination can motivate us so that we are more likely to achieve and reach a goal or an ambition.

Sports men and women are taught what is widely called 'visualisation', the controlled creation of constructive and positive images in the mind, the purpose being to make those images become real. I have worked with several such individuals and their imaginations, to help them overcome bouts of uncertainty, where their performance has fallen away for some reason. Without fail, where the individual works at the process and is consistent, the improvements do come. Goals are scored, 'personal bests' are surpassed, and levels of attainment are generally lifted.

These ideas are not new. They are in fact very old. Before

Staying Cool

mankind had developed written languages as we have them today, knowledge, ideas and traditions were passed on through stories (sound) and the images they create (imagination) in the mind. There were no textbooks, so stories were told, sung and imagined and given from one generation to another, stored in the picture boxes that exist in the mental filing cabinet, waiting to be shared with the next generation. The storyteller and the troubadour were important figures in societies where literacy was rare.

Great leaders and generals used their words to inspire others, as they wove marvellous ideas and images in the minds of those followers who were listening to them. Winston Churchill did this to great effect in the Second World War as he sought to inspire the British people in difficult times.

And a great story writer or poet will use words to stimulate images, pictures and the feelings that accompany them, so that the reader travels with them into another world, another place.

In an age of television, videos, computer games and so on, this imagining facility, so important for us all, has become a little more passive. We frequently tend to be spectators. As mentioned earlier, a play or drama on the radio has to be much more descriptive than if it takes place on television or film. We can't see what is going on, so we need more dialogue, more words, and usually more sound effects to help us understand what is happening. However, another, positive aspect of listening to a sound-only story like a radio play or commentary is the stimulus it gives to our minds and imagination. It is a very creative form of mental exercise, encouraging our inner picture box to build and make pictures. We become part of the process, we participate and our experience can be all the more dramatic and powerful because of that.

Images in Your Mind

If you had stories read to you as a child cast your mind back to those times. Remember the stories and the pictures you drew in your imagination and how you responded to them. Somewhere in your mental filing cabinet, those pictures are stored, and you can recall many of them if you try.

Take a little pause and think of a favourite story from years ago, one that was read to you, perhaps, or one you read as a young child that made a strong impact upon you. Recall the colours, the shapes, the characters, and the places in which the events of the story took place. As some of the pictures come to you, allow them to become stronger and clearer. Inside your head, your imagination will weave its magic and show you how you were creative at that time.

You built those pictures, painted those colours; you may even feel again the sensations you experienced as the pictures and images developed and changed: the happy parts of the story, the exciting parts, the moments of tension and relief, the moments of suspense and the moments of wonder.

You had an unlimited picture box in your mind to create whatever you wanted to. That was your imagination working for you, and it is still with you, as wonderful as ever.

Creating Calm Space

The earlier exercises will give you a basis on which to become calm, *staying cool, calm and collected*.

However, developing your imagination in a relaxed state will enhance your life, your effectiveness, your performance and success in so many ways.

Here is a simple way to create a calm space, a place you can go to whenever you want to, wherever you are, so that you can return to everyday activity more alert and powerful, more at ease, and with a clearer mind.

Key Exercise: Calm Space – An Inner Garden

1. Sit quietly where you will not be disturbed. Put any thoughts or concerns you may have floating around in your busy mind, into your old friend, your mental suitcase.
2. Close your eyes, if you have not done so already and develop the slow rhythm in your breath as you have done before. Slow and easy, think to yourself, 'I breathe in,' pause, 'I breathe out.'
3. Remember the light above your head, and let it flow through you in a wave as you did before. Again, slowly, build the picture in your mind of this gentle, calming light flowing downwards, filling your entire body, from head to feet, from your shoulders out to your hands.
4. Now, slowly bring your attention upwards to the space inside your head where your imagination builds the pictures. This is just behind your forehead, underneath the crown of your head. It is your private cinema screen, where you can watch whatever images you like.
5. Imagine that a beautiful garden appears in front of you, with a small garden gate, waiting for you to open it. Open the gate and take yourself into the garden, to have a stroll around.

6. Let the pictures grow. Let the garden develop and you can put anything into it, just like painting a picture. Make it warm, quiet and beautiful with everything you wish to imagine. You may also like to hear sounds: birds, crickets, perhaps frogs jumping into a pond. Look at the flowers; they are very, very healing for you to be with. You may even smell the perfumes of the flowers, and feel the warmth of the sun on your face. Build this calm, beautiful, happy picture and enjoy doing so.
7. Find somewhere to sit down in this garden. Relax and enjoy it. This is a special calm place that is entirely yours. Others cannot come here, unless you allow them to. In this garden you have just what you want to have. Enjoy the peace and the calm for a few moments. Think to yourself a few times, 'I am really calm here. Really, really calm.'
8. When you feel ready to, you can leave your garden and return through the little gate you opened before. Let the image fade gradually.
9. Slowly bring your attention back to the room you are sitting in, noticing the gentle rhythm in your breathing, around your solar plexus area.
10. Think of your feet touching the floor, grounding yourself carefully, before slowly opening your eyes.

Remember, always come out of the exercises slowly. Then, when you are fully awake, you can go about your normal activities.

I use the words *slowly, gently, gradually* often. In our frantic world, where we are encouraged to rush around, chasing here and there, it is important to conduct ourselves in a more considered, balanced way. The use of these words will help you, not only in benefiting from the exercises in this book, but also to live life generally at a more even pace. Of course, there are times when we need to act quickly, but we also need to be controlled and calm when we can choose to be. This will help you stay cool and calm.

The garden you created is your calm space, a place you can go to at any time to be still, be happy, to just enjoy some calm in a busy world. In one school where we did this exercise, a young student said, 'My Mum could do with a calm space like mine!' I suggested he teach it to her. I don't know if he did!

As well as relaxing you, and releasing excess stress from your body and mind, this exercise will also encourage your imagination and stimulate your creativity.

If you don't fancy having a garden as a calm space, you can try some other ideas.

Key Exercise: Calm Space – A Quiet Room

Try the same exercise, but this time, when you get to step 5 (page 90), instead of a garden, picture a door leading into a quiet, warm, comfortable room.

- Open the door of your room, walk inside, and see it decorated and furnished comfortably, just how you would wish it to be. Allow your imagination to work.
- The lighting in the room is very restful, very calming. It may be full of candles or other soft lights.
- Sit and rest in your room for a few moments, before returning out through the door.
- Focus on your solar plexus and your rhythmic breathing as before, ground yourself and open your eyes slowly as you return.

You may notice that in both these suggestions for your *calm space* I have asked you to open a gate or a door. The reason is that your subconscious mind will receive a message from this. The opening of a door or gate, or the stepping through into a clearing in a wood, will take you into a more relaxed state, into a deeper, calmer level of yourself where everything is more peaceful and tranquil. The doors or gates tell the subconscious that is what you wish to do, and the more you practise the exercise, the more it will help you. It is a kind of training at which you will get better and better, the more you go through it all.

Key Exercise: Calm Space – A Starry Sky

Work through steps 1–4 as before (page 90), then:
- Imagine yourself to be outside on a cliff top near to the sea, on a quiet starlit night. See the beautiful stars and a bright clear moon that illuminates the space all around you. In the background you can hear the waves of the sea.
- There is a safe gentle pathway running down the cliff which is lit up by the moonlight. Walk down it carefully and slowly, until your feet touch the soft sand of the beach.
- Find somewhere to sit as you look up at the stars, all the way out to the horizon. You may see the lights of one or two ships in the distance, and notice how the moonlight seems to paint the waves silver as they break gently on a calm sea. Enjoy it. You are safe, comfortable and calm here.
- When you have stayed for a while and you will know when you wish to come back, walk back up to the top of the cliff, pausing when you reach the top, to stand in the bright moonlight.

- Then return slowly as you have done before, grounding yourself and opening your eyes slowly.

In this visualisation, you didn't have a door, or a gate, but instead you walked down the steps of the cliff to the beach. This also has the effect of taking you deeper into your relaxation, your calmness.

A Calm Space – You Do It!

If these suggestions don't seem to be right for you or you wish to try others, then be creative and invent a calm inner space for yourself. Be your own 'inner artist' and follow the principles here, creating something of your own.

The important things to remember are as follows:
- Work through steps 1–4 (page 90) before using your imagination.
- Try to put in the idea of opening 'into' your inner space. Give it a door, a gate, some steps, stairs; go into a clearing in a wood or whatever. Move from one space to another to reach your *calm space*.
- Always come out as you go in to the calm space, and then return to your rhythmic breathing, grounding through your feet, and gradually opening your eyes.

You may like to do a drawing of your *calm space* at some point. This isn't for everyone, but some readers may like the idea and it will reinforce the process in your mind. If you'd rather, you could describe it in words. Perhaps write a poem about it. It is up to you, a kind of optional extra.

Practise with these ideas, and a *commitment* to see them through will pay enormous dividends to you, and when you develop a good strong picture of your calm space, you can also call upon it at any time, in any situation, quickly. You can tap into it briefly in a moment of tension or anxiety, simply by thinking of it and briefly calling the picture into your mind. And you will become calm at once. A vivid and well-constructed image or picture can call forth a remarkable and powerful reaction in you.

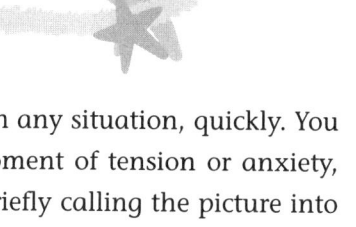

One example of this is the logo or brand-mark. Manufacturers of products spend vast sums of money and use lots of creative energy to come up with symbols and images that we can all see, quickly and immediately.

If you cast your mind around the clothes you like, the foods and drink you prefer, the cars and hi-fi of your choice, most if not all of them will quickly bring an image and logo or brand-mark into your mind, with the accompanying idea and feeling such as

'I like that'
or
'They are good'
or
'That looks cool'
and quite possibly,
'I want one of those'.

Whilst we can question the morality or desirability of these images manipulating us, equally, you can create images and ideas in your mind that can influence, calm and if necessary motivate you, so you can give of your best in all situations and circumstances. And remember, a calm you is a powerful, more effective you.

At a recent course I gave in Scotland, a student informed me of a situation where a powerful image she had learned from one of my cassette tapes helped her through a difficult experience. Some years ago she was driving her car when she skidded on a patch of wet leaves. Her car spun off the road and crashed into a fence, and a large fence post smashed through her windscreen, almost hitting her in the face. When she finally came to, the top of the post was jutting through the windscreen just an inch or so from her eyes, and she was very fortunate not to have sustained serious facial injury.

Consequently, she suffered from severe shock, which manifested itself predominantly as an inability to get off to sleep. The images of the accident surfaced as she closed her eyes at night. Her daughter bought one of my self-help cassettes, which is designed to help people who cannot sleep well. The powerful images developed in her mind when listening to the recording enabled her to sleep, initially using the cassette tape, but after just three nights, she could do it without the cassette. And she has been okay ever since. Whenever she had a recurrence of the problem in the months immediately following the accident, she would call the images to mind and the calm state for sleep would return.

Success Visualisation

You can use your imaging capacity to improve your performance in all manner of things: in sport, in music or drama, in taking a test or examination. By taking a pause, being calm and using your imagination with both sides of your brain closely synchronised, you can gear up your mind and body for the best possible outcome.

All it takes is a consistent, powerful image in a relaxed mode, repeated regularly. The improvements will certainly come.

Sport

Visualisation will obviously not replace all the sensible training and coaching needed for effective performance in any sport. You have to follow the suggested training and fitness regime, and listen to your coach or trainer's tactics, whatever the sport you participate in. But it can help you considerably.

Applying the technique to sport, it is good to practise success visualisation once or twice a week as follows.

1. Take a pause, breathe deeply and rhythmically for a few moments as you learned to do in the key unstressing exercises earlier on.
2. Using your imagination, fill your body with energy, allowing the energy to flow from your head to your toes.
3. When you have done the above, which should take 5 minutes or so, lift your attention upwards until you are in your imagination, the space just behind your brow energy centre, and beneath your crown. Here you can imagine anything at all.
4. Before you build your picture, say your name inside your mind. Then think the sport you wish to focus on, for example football, cricket, rugby, or tennis.
5. Now encourage the picture to form in your imagination of you dressed for the sport. See this picture as clearly as you can. It may take practice, but work at it. It will be worth all the effort.
6. Now begin to see yourself *active* in the sport.

If it is football, imagine yourself enjoying your game, really in the flow of it. You can even imagine a commentary as if the game is being televised or filmed. You are both player and commentator. 'Alan Jones is playing well here.

Staying Cool

He passes the ball well.' If there is something you need to improve upon in your game, imagine that happening in particular.

- See yourself scoring goals, tackling well and winning the ball.
- See yourself passing the ball, taking good corners, free kicks.

Go through whatever you feel is important for you to be successful and that will help you to enjoy improving your performance.

If it is athletics, imagine yourself showing perfect technique, running powerfully, jumping high or long as is necessary. Again, be the commentator. 'Anna is running beautifully, so fast, so full of power', and so on.

Whatever the sport you are interested in, think of what you need to accomplish and see yourself succeeding. In tennis or squash, you can observe your fine strokes and volleys. In rugby you can enjoy imagining scoring tries, passing and catching well, making good tackles.

Remember the following rules:

- **Always imagine a good general performance first, and then be specific and focus on a particular skill or technique that you wish to develop or improve.**
- **Always see yourself succeeding.**
- **Always see yourself being congratulated.**
- **Always have a commentary in your mind.**
- **Always be relaxed first.**

Your Imagination

I used these techniques with a couple of footballers. One was having difficulty in scoring goals so we worked on the unstressing techniques, along with him using his imagination to build a picture of himself playing well and scoring goals. Gradually his confidence returned and his game improved. He returned to his goal-scoring ways.

Earlier on, I mentioned the energy centres and the solar plexus. The first judgement of space we make is in the solar plexus centre. We use this to literally 'feel' our space, and footballers, along with other sports men and women, use the solar plexus all the time. Some great players have a very sensitive solar plexus area. Paul Gascoigne and George Best are two examples. They had wonderful ball skills, but instead of managing to keep the solar plexus calm as you will have done by unstressing and staying cool techniques, they resorted to other methods of inducing relaxation, such as alcohol. However, such techniques work only temporarily and produce other more serious problems later on.

So, learn to unstress first, become calm, and then visualise.

Another footballer was trying to take more accurate corner kicks. He felt his technique was far too erratic as some of his kicks were good; others though were not. I told him to imagine success with his kicks, to see them going where he wished them to go. I also advised him to imagine that there were invisible channels along which he could slot the ball, to any spot he wished. Before the visualisation, his success rate was around 50/50, half good, half not so good. Immediately after visualisation, he improved this to around 70/80 per cent accuracy. This was achieved in minutes. He was amazed!

With regular, continuous practice of this technique, the

skill will become easier and easier for you; it will become more consistent and reliable. Then you will need to simply think the idea and you will have access to it. Of course, you will have to keep fit too! But once learned and practised, these techniques become more immediate and easier for you!

The imagination both encourages and prepares the body for what it has to do to develop the skill. The imagination process you are learning here will give you the perfect balance between relaxation and alertness, both in your physical body and in your mind, that you need for effective performance.

Examination Success

You can also use these techniques to work towards goals of success in tests, examinations and career. Before an exam or test, imagine success. Develop a picture in your mind of yourself, relaxed and writing or drawing carefully, with a happy expression on your face.

Perhaps build an image of yourself happy and smiling, holding the results in your hand as your success is confirmed in results.

Be aware that the vision in your imagination has to accompany hard, constructive work. There is no substitute for that. But the imagination can help you to make the most of what you have learned and what you have studied.

Apparent Failures – Being Patient

As you move towards success, remember that it may take time. Although sometimes results are immediate, it more often takes time and patience for the success to unfold. It is also possible that you may experience some failures on the way to your success; in fact we can learn a lot from the failures and difficulties we experience, by discovering where and why we went wrong or what we need to improve upon, or what knowledge we still need to acquire. Sometimes the lesson of failure is more obscure and becomes clear to us later.

But patient persistence will be helped wonderfully by the imagination. And it, in turn, will help you to get where you wish to be, in a smooth, calm way.

Performance

In performance of other kinds, perhaps acting or singing, again you can do some long-term visualisation. Here, you can imagine yourself acting with perfect ease and intensity. Picture yourself on the stage, acting your role with style and receiving the applause of the audience. Singers and musicians can do the same. In your relaxed mind, create the pictures of success and they will help to get you there.

I ran courses for actors some years ago. Many actors do use their inner vision and imagination well, but some don't use it effectively and restrict the success and fulfilment they could enjoy. If you are a performer, see yourself performing well and hear the quality of your performance in your head – wonderful tones, perfect clarity of words and so on. Live the successful performance in your imagination and that is what you will achieve.

The Quick Vision

As well as developing your vision of success as I have described, to be practised once or twice a week in a deeply relaxed state, you can also use the 'Quick Vision' before you

undertake the task you have been training or rehearsing for.
- Whilst you are waiting in your dressing room to go on stage, you can quickly call to mind your image of success. You may not have time to enter deep relaxation, but you don't need to for this.
- For a quick vision, once you have practised the deeper technique for a while, you can simply close your eyes and call up the images.
- Smile as you do so and all the earlier efforts working with your imagination will pay off and the picture will form easily for you. This will help you to focus, be calm and confident and perform wonderfully.

You can use the Quick Vision in sport, exams, interviews, driving tests and any situation you wish. You will be surprised how well it works. I cannot promise that you will win every race you enter, score in every match, act with the ease of Tom Hanks, or sing like your favourite singer. But you will improve and experience the success you need to feel satisfied, fulfilled and have a desire to go on to greater and greater things.

Reach for the stars. It is your right to do so, if you wish to, whilst being patient with yourself as you grow and develop.

Clearing a Sadness, Clearing a Failure

You will inevitably at some time experience a little failure. We all do so, and we become stronger and wiser for overcoming such disappointments. If you experience sadness or disappointment that seems to stay around, do speak to family, friends, teachers and those you trust so that they are aware of how you feel.

- **Never bottle up unhappy feelings that won't go away.**
- **Share them with your family, friends or teachers.**
- **Find someone you can trust to talk to. There is always someone.**

However, there are techniques you can employ to release such feelings. I suggest two here that I have used with young people over the last 15 years.

The Three Steps

1. Sit quietly for a while and go through the unstressing exercise in Chapter 2 so that you feel relaxed and calm.
2. Our unhappiness and sadness tends to settle in the same place as our fear, in the solar plexus area. So briefly imagine the subject or cause of your sadness to be in your solar plexus, near to your stomach area.
3. Imagine it to be a ball of colour, perhaps a little dark and heavy.

Step One
Imagine this colour moving slowly upwards until it reaches your heart area. As it moves upwards, imagine the colour becoming lighter. The feeling also becomes a little lighter, less intense.

Step Two
Now you see your ball of colour as it rises up slowly from your heart into your head, again the colour becoming

lighter and clearer. The ball will be much brighter and you also will feel much brighter inside.

Step Three
Imagine the ball of colour now floating away from you, upwards, out of you and away as if it is a balloon, carried on the wind. It is gone and it has left you. Inside your head, say 'It is gone.'

4. Then gradually return from this exercise by concentrating for a few minutes on your breathing, slowly and rhythmically, as you have done in earlier exercises.
5. Ground yourself through your feet before you open your eyes.

You may have to repeat this exercise a few times before you feel free from the feeling of sadness or failure. That is okay and normal, as your subconscious needs, sometimes at least, a few reminders from you, what it is you want. But it will eventually do as you and your imagination tells it to.

So again, be patient with yourself and give things a little time to improve. They will.

If it is a sadness of some deep nature, do seek help. We are all here to help each other, if only we realise it! Don't try to do everything on your own. These exercises will help, but they can't replace good advice and a listening ear.

If you are clearing a sense of failure, then it is good after practising these exercises to do something very positive, something constructive. Do something you enjoy and do it well. It doesn't matter what it is, so long as it is practical and positive.

Your Imagination

Dance, sing, paint, draw, have a game of tennis, take another driving lesson, play some football. It doesn't have to be dramatic or vast. Simply do it. You will feel good afterwards and it will help you to clear the feeling of sadness or failure, by building up creative energy in you again.

Another way to release a sense of failure, disappointment or a general feeling of being down is this simple version of the 'Ten Finger' technique taught earlier.

Key Exercise: Fingers and Thumbs

1. First, simply close your eyes and imagine a time when you were very happy. It may have been when you were on holiday with friends or family, or perhaps had received news of some success.
2. Imagine the occasion and, most important, remember how you felt at that time.

Visualise success.

3. As you see the event and feel the good, happy feeling, press tightly the tips of your index fingers and thumbs. Smile as you do this.
4. Really revel in this, make it as powerful as you can, then let it all go. Practise this exercise a few times, until you have it firmly in your mind.

Now, once you have practised this, you have a wonderful tool at your disposal, a tool that will help you to clear any negative, unhappy feeling.

When a sadness or feeling, or memory of failure enters your mind:

- Pause from what you are doing, when it is reasonably safe or convenient to do so.
- Press together your fingers and thumbs and feel the smile and good feeling rise up in you, clearing the negative, unhappy sense in you as it does so.

After a few moments, the sensation will lift and you will feel better, more positive and able to go on with your normal tasks or activities in a clearer frame of mind.

I have made this 'Fingers and Thumbs' a Key Exercise; it is something I think everyone should learn, for like other Key Exercises, it has a broad and generally useful effect and application.

You can use this exercise in any situation. Before a test or exam, or simply when feeling unhappy, afraid of something or of the unknown. It needs practice first of all, so that the link between pressing the finger and thumb and the happy, positive feeling is firmly established in your mind. But once it is fixed in there, it will work well for you every time!

Your Imagination

A Word about Causes of Sadness

Sometimes we don't know why we feel sad. In our busy world, full of demands and pressures, we can sometimes feel 'down in the dumps' for no apparent or easily identifiable reason.

It may be that we are tired. Often when we are young, quite naturally we wish to keep going as long as we can, all day and all night if possible. My own children were like that (one of them still is!).

Make sure you get plenty of sleep. When you are growing physically, you need a lot of rest and sleep. Lack of sleep can make us briefly unhappy, even slightly depressed.

Eat well. Fruits and vegetables are particularly important in keeping a clear mind and positive attitude, so eat plenty of them as part of a balanced diet.

Also, as we grow, there are the biological changes which can be perplexing and certainly affect how we experience our feelings. Non-specific sadness, where we don't seem to know the cause, usually passes with a balanced approach to life: good diet, good regular exercise, plenty of rest and sleep and a fair balance between the work we must do and the bits of fun so necessary from time to time. We'll look at that later.

But if you have persistent sadness, and you don't know why, then seek advice and support through your family, teachers and where necessary, your doctor. Don't let it linger. Why should you? You are special. Life needs you, and needs you happy.

Sometimes we know why we are sad. It can be that we

have split with our boyfriend or girlfriend and we feel empty, disappointed and let down. We can be sad because someone we love is ill, or may even die. We feel powerless, wishing we could do more to help that person.

It may be that we fail badly in something where others are succeeding and we then feel hopeless, useless and inferior. 'They are all so good, so clever, so beautiful – yet I'm not.' This can bring loneliness to us, a sense of isolation, a feeling that life has somehow picked us out for rotten luck and poor treatment. We can even be overwhelmed by our sadness for a while. Life can seem so unfair and painful in moments such as these.

When we feel sad, we should not feel guilty about it. Moments and periods of sadness nearly always pass and things eventually brighten up for us. And we learn a lot from these situations as we overcome them.

And even the shedding of tears can be a release and can help us to cast off our worst, most hurt feelings. If we feel sad because of the problems of someone we love and care for, then we should do what we can to help that person, remembering that 'being there' is the most important help we can give. Often it is not only what we say, or what we actually do, that is so important. It is our constructive, helpful and cheerful presence that can make a difference. We have to be strong, positive and happy for those around us – family, friends and colleagues – when they need us to be.

One 17-year-old boy asked me what he could do for his girlfriend. She was extremely depressed and although getting help from her doctor and school, she had still tried to harm herself several times. He was very worried and he said to me, 'How can I help her?' I told him to be strong and, at the same time, loving and caring. She needed him 'to be there' for her during this crisis, so he should take care of himself, keep himself as calm and positive as he could, and that would help her immeasurably. His calm, constructive and caring presence was a great gift he could give to her.

Breaking Up

Breaking up with a boyfriend or girlfriend can be extremely painful. Our confidence and trust may be broken and we feel rejected. Or we may be guilty because of the hurt we feel we have caused. These experiences really hurt. And it seems that we can never get over them. We go off our food, cannot concentrate, think the whole world is looking (and maybe laughing) at us. We may lose interest in things we normally enjoyed. But this passes: it always does and the deep feelings in the solar plexus eventually clear away. We have to give it time and be easy on ourselves at such sad times, knowing that the hurt and any guilt we feel will fade. Again, seek help from a counsellor, teacher, friend or member of your family. Talk to those around you who seek to help you. Don't reject them. They are only doing what you would do to help another in a bad time or difficult moment.

Research in the USA showed that people who are ill and who also discussed their feelings and concerns with others, recovered more quickly than those who kept things to themselves. When we are sad because of our circumstances, because of things that have happened or are happening to us, then we should seek help. Where you know what is making you sad, take what sensible actions you can to eliminate it from your life, or put right what you know you can put right.

Remember, you are sensible, imaginative and will know what to do. Where you cannot change things straight away, use the techniques in this book. They will help you considerably to grow stronger and calmer. Things will change, and will improve, and the sadness will eventually fade.

Always think and act in a calm and unstressed way, and stay cool.

A Visualisation for Clearing Sadness

This little exercise may help you to let go of a sad idea, especially one that lingers.

1. First of all, gently rub your calves and the lower part of your legs and your feet for a few moments.
2. Close your eyes and begin to breathe slowly and deeply, focusing upon the movement of your solar plexus and stomach area.
3. When your breath has slowed down, imagine, in your solar plexus, there is a large bucket, full to the top with water.
4. Into this bucket, you drop all the sad ideas and thoughts you have. Imagine them dropping into the water, like tear drops.
5. Next, you tip the bucket and allow the water, containing all the sad thoughts, to pour downwards through your legs and feet, and away into the ground, leaving your body completely. Think the words 'I let go of sadness now. It's washed away.' The bucket is now empty, and you can put it away. You may use it again later on if you feel you need to, as many times as you wish.
6. Now focus again upon your breathing, and imagine a beautiful, golden sun appearing, where the bucket was, deep in your solar plexus.

7. Allow this sun to radiate its bright warmth throughout your body, and as it does so, it will fill you with safe, good feelings.
8. Finally, slowly open your eyes and return to normal consciousness.

It may be that during this exercise, you shed one or two tears around your eyes, that don't make it into the bucket. That's okay. They will disappear too.

A Deeper Meditation – The Benefits

Much has been researched about the effects of deep relaxation and meditation, and we have already considered some of the benefits.

Various threads of research throughout the world have indicated that a diverse range of benefits follows from deep relaxation and meditation: a measurable improvement in intelligence rating or IQ (Intelligence Quotient), greater creativity, improved memory and comprehension, along with the physical benefits of stress reduction (including lower blood pressure), a decrease in cigarette, alcohol and drug dependency and abuse; in fact, a general reduction in the need for medical care.

Research in the USA has shown that meditation produces a significantly larger reduction in tobacco, alcohol and illicit drug use than standard substance abuse treatments or prevention programmes, designed to counteract peer group pressures and promote individual personality development (*International Journal of Addiction* 1991; *Alcoholism Treatment Quarterly* 1987).

Deep breathing and meditation has also been shown to improve general fitness. The medical journal *The Lancet* of May 1998 published research indicating that the deeper, slower breathing rates, developed in meditational practices, increase the levels of oxygen in the blood stream considerably, enabling individuals to perform better on exercise tests. The report concludes that deep breathing benefits the respiratory muscles, especially the heart, and enhances physical exercise potential and fitness in general.

So, deep breathing and meditation not only unstresses you and makes you calmer and clearer in your mind, it also makes you fitter in your body!

Meditation is the deeper state we experience as we relax deeply, become calm and then go through the brain wave patterns we discussed earlier, through beta and alpha to theta and beyond.

A Deeper Relaxation and Meditation Technique

Here is a process that some of you may wish to try. It will help you benefit from very deep relaxation and meditative states. You will benefit from it most if you have already practised the unstressing exercises and are reasonably able to slip into the rhythmic breathing pattern that is central to it.

I have taught this for many years. To derive most benefit, it is best practised daily, for at least 10 minutes at a time, one session a day for a minimum of 4 weeks, along with any other techniques you may try.

When you first practise, it may well take you more than 10 minutes, but once you are familiar with the process, that will be sufficient.

Your Imagination

Take yourself away from distractions, noise, take a pause and follow this process:

1. Close your eyes. Place any ideas or thoughts on your mind into your mental suitcase. It is bottomless so you can put as much as you like into it!
2. Focus on your solar plexus area and establish slow, deep rhythmic breathing. If you have already been practising, you can slow this down considerably and comfortably, to five or six times per minute (the average normal 'resting' rate of breathing for an individual is around 12–14 times per minute).
3. Allow this slow, deep rhythm to be the centre of your attention. Think of nothing other than breathing. Allow yourself to be completely absorbed into your breathing and the movement in your solar plexus area.
4. As you feel more and more calm, slowly imagine that your whole body is breathing. Think this idea: 'My entire body is breathing. My entire body is calm.'
5. After a few moments, allow your attention to float gently up to your head, resting in the space in the centre of your head, behind your eyes, beneath the crown of your head.
6. Imagine a small point of coloured light in your forehead. (At first, it may take a little while to form, but with practice it will form immediately.) Try to keep your breath slow and rhythmic as this light develops and grows until you feel a beautiful, clear, comfortable glow inside your head.
7. After a few moments, allow the light to fade and disappear. Then float your attention down to your solar plexus. Do it gently and slowly.
8. Cease concentrating on your breathing and focus upon

your feet, grounding yourself. Think of the room around you and slowly open your eyes. Sit still for a few moments to re-orientate yourself before going about your normal daily activities.

In the practice of this meditation, you will develop very wonderful deep states of calm and peacefulness which you can tap into throughout your day as you choose to.

The breathing will become easier and more effective. And the beautiful light in your head will help you to feel clear, bright and mentally alert. This light will grow and develop with practice. Just go with what you experience. It will be very beautiful and safe. Be patient and allow it to form and unfold as it surely will.

Summary of Activities

- *Key Exercise: A Calm Space*

Learn to create a calm space, a location or 'place' in your imagination that you can visit as you please. You can visit
- An inner garden
- A quiet room
- A starry sky by the sea

or a vision of your own making. Reinforce the idea with a sketch or drawing.

- *Success Visualisation*

Develop the skill of using your imagination to achieve goals, to work towards improvement and success in any area of your life: sport, performances, tests and so on.

- *Quick Vision*

Practise brief moments where you close your eyes,

Your Imagination

summoning up a 'quick', powerful image of your success moments before you perform or face a challenging situation.

- *Clearing a Sadness, Clearing a Failure*

Along with any counselling or guidance you seek, develop relaxation techniques to clear the thoughts and ideas that connect with sadness and the disappointments that come your way, so that you can move on and achieve all you wish to achieve.

> *Three Steps Method* Lifting the changing colour representing the idea from the solar plexus to the heart, to the head and then completely away from you.
>
> *Key Exercise: Fingers and Thumbs* Learn to connect with positive, happy feelings and use them to replace the negative ones in your mind, as you press together your fingers and your thumbs.

- *A Visualisation for Clearing Sadness*

This is a little exercise to help you clear a sadness that tends to linger, as you put the sad ideas into a bucket and pour them away.

- *A Deeper Relaxation and Meditation Technique*

Practise the deep rhythmic technique until your whole body seems to breathe with deep relaxation, before developing a clear light in your head. This is a beautiful technique to practise regularly for those who wish to experience deeper meditation and experience the benefits of it.

Chapter 5
Happy and Positive

Having a Laugh

The healing effects of humour and laughter are becoming increasingly well documented and researched, and many therapists use laughter as an important aspect of healing. 'Laughter Therapy' is now also coming into use in more orthodox situations, such as hospitals and clinics.

The work of American doctor Patch Adams is now very famous and he has done much ground-breaking work in the use of laughter amongst patients, especially children, to help them cope with life and the stresses and strains of illnesses and disease and often with difficult treatments. If you haven't already seen it, I recommend that you watch the film of his life, 'Patch Adams', starring Robin Williams as Patch himself. It is a very interesting and humorous movie based on his attempts to bring a more human and caring face into medicine and generally helping people to feel good and worthwhile.

The Smile Count

One day, when you are perhaps walking around town, or maybe sitting waiting in a busy airport or bus station, pause for 5 minutes and watch the faces of the people as they walk around, pass by or sit and wait.

See how many of them are actually smiling. Watch the faces and count how many smiles you can see. You may be lucky and see several smiles, maybe a real chuckle or laugh, but the chances are that most people will be carrying serious expressions and many may even be frowning. Next, do a 'frown count'. Most often you will see and count far more frowns than smiles.

Now, I'm not suggesting that in all situations we should grin inanely like the Cheshire cat. But what I am suggesting is that we can smile far more often than we do, and that smiling helps us in so many ways, more than we realise. Smiling can help you. In fact, when we smile, we use far fewer facial muscles than when we frown. In other words, smiling takes far less effort than frowning. That alone is one good reason to smile more often.

And smiling people are more attractive. I know a salesman who is very, very successful. He is, of course, good at his job in the usually accepted ways, but he has something extra. People like to see him, including his customers, because he smiles a lot, and not with a kind of superficial grimace that fools no one, but with a real smile that comes from the heart. He also likes people, pays people compliments and always has a joke or two to tell. He has his serious moments too, as we all have, but it is not long before a smile spreads across his face.

The Smile Technique
1. Take a little pause.
2. Think of something that makes you happy, some very positive, happy idea. It may be something from your

past, the memory of a special occasion, perhaps a favourite joke that always makes you grin or something from a movie. Whatever it is, call it to mind for a moment.
3. As you do so, focus your attention upon your face muscles.
4. Observe them. If they haven't done so already, they will try to form a smile, maybe even a laugh.
5. Let the good feeling spread. Let it spread all over you so that your whole body feels as if it is connected to your smile.

Notice how you feel. Not only will you begin to feel happier and more positive, you will also start to release stresses and tensions that may be in you or around you.

I'm sure you can think of occasions when a bit of humour and laughter was able to lighten tensions or disperse a bad atmosphere. Try to ensure that you do things that produce happiness for you and the people with whom you come in contact. It is a very important idea.

As I said earlier, smiling, happy people are more attractive and are more likely to be successful in life, as well as being healthier and less tense.

In his book *Anatomy of an Illness*, Norman Cousins tells of his own recovery from serious illness, achieved largely by watching a continuous stream of movies that made him laugh and laugh. Keep books and videos that make you laugh and that you can read or watch occasionally, especially when you need cheering up or you are tired or under pressure.

I like joke books. I have several on my shelves and from time to time I pull one off the shelf and have a smile at the contents. Use smiling and laughter as an unstressing tool, and see if you can ensure that it is in your life regularly.

Smiling radiates good energy, however black things seem.

Smile Day

Choose a day as a 'smile day'. It may sound a bit crazy, but try it as an experiment. Nominate a day (and the sooner the better) where you are going to remember the good feelings of laughter and smiling.

Write on a card or small piece of paper: 'Today is a smile day. I shall smile rather than frown.' During the course of the day, at appropriate moments, be aware of your face muscles. If they are heavy, tight and frowning, then briefly call to mind your smile technique, press your finger and thumb together and then smile gently. You will have a wonderful effect upon the people around you. You watch and see. And you will have a positive effect upon yourself too.

Of course, there are moments when smiling is perhaps not deemed appropriate, such as being told off by a parent or teacher, or when someone is distressed or in pain.

But make an effort to smile more during every day and

you will feel better yourself and others around you will also feel better. When we are children, although we cry with frustration sometimes, we are much more willing to smile. As we get older we seem to forget how to do it.

Re-learn it. Make a pact with yourself to smile more and remember the things that make you happy and that make you laugh. And if you have some favourite jokes, or someone tells you a happy, funny story, you may wish to note it down, so you can call it to mind later on. It's your own joke book or list. You don't have to share it with anyone else unless you wish to. It's for you. And anyway, someone else's sense of what is funny may be different to yours.

What Have I Achieved?

It is very important to be constructive and positive about ourselves, to value who we are. It is very important that you have a good and positive vision of yourself – self-image it is called.

Now the unstressing and meditational exercises, if practised over a period of time, will in themselves help you to develop self-esteem and an improved sense of self-worth. Being positive about yourself does not mean being aggressive or big-headed. People who behave in such ways are usually sending out a different message and simply trying to mask feelings of insecurity.

Constructive, positive individuals are usually calm, pleasant and fairly happy with themselves and their lives. They approach situations with an open mind, willing to give of their best, not afraid to work hard, sometimes succeeding, sometimes having to pause, regroup and try again.

Happy and Positive

And people who are constructive and positive about themselves and their lives are more attractive and popular. There is nothing worse than a miserable person, who always sees the worst in things, and is very critical.

A recent research study at the University of Hertford, UK, conducted by Dr Richard Wiseman, shows that positive, optimistic people have more 'good luck' than others and that we can actually attract more good fortune by developing constructive, happy attitudes.

In the 'Smile Technique' I suggested that you use an affirmation. It is a positive statement of intent, that we wish and intend to make real.

'Every day in every way I get better and better' is an affirmation or positive statement designed to help us to re-programme our thinking and create constructive, positive ideas in our minds.

As part of an over-all programme of unstressing and learning how to take charge of our lives, with positive attitudes, affirmations can be very useful. They help us to re-programme our thinking.

- They can help us to think positively about ourselves.
- They can also help us to think constructively about others and our circumstances.
- They can help us to achieve goals and be calmly determined and confident.
- Cool, Calm and Confident – the three 'Cs' – what a powerful combination you can exude.

Remember that confident people are calm people. Calm people are confident, more self-assured.

Smile in embarrassing moments.

Challenge and Problem

A common change in language today which is an indication of how positive thinking techniques have infiltrated our consciousness is the use of the word 'challenge' instead of 'problem'. I do this often in my writing and teaching.

The word problem has taken on increasingly negative connotations. The idea of a problem is something that can seem huge and daunting, a difficult task we face, tinged with doubt and fear about our relationship to it.

A problem can seem huge, like a huge wall with no ladder before us. So, many people gradually have swapped the word 'problem' for that of 'challenge'. The word challenge is somehow seen as less threatening, smaller, more accessible. 'A challenge' has a sporty flavour about it, indicating that it is not so serious. It we call a problem a challenge, we are immediately suggesting that victory of some kind lies ahead if we stick to our guns and if we don't give up.

Positive people are winners. They never give up. They don't have problems. They have challenges. They take up the challenge and eventually succeed.

Happy and Positive

There are many stories of people who experienced failure, problems or difficulties, but who, through positive thinking and determination have succeeded. I read many biographies and autobiographies, and I never cease to be amazed at how persistence and a calm determination will always ultimately lead to success.

Calm determination will <u>always</u> lead to success,
- **If there is something you wish to improve**
- **If there is something you wish to achieve.**

Not only *can* you achieve it, but you *will* achieve it if you stick with it and never give up.

Many years ago I taught in a large grammar school. I had one pupil who was a little rebellious and this was largely because he struggled in a school where academic achievement was paramount. Whilst he was intelligent, he was not naturally inclined to study. He found it difficult and he was one of the lower achievers. One day, in a lesson, he confided in me about his future. He told me he loved cars, he really enjoyed tinkering with them and his dad had taught him some basic rudimentary mechanics. 'I want my own garage. I'd really like to do that,' he said to me.

Like most of us, when he was motivated, he could do well. He played rugby for the school and showed great determination on the sports field where he achieved much success. 'If you want to, you can do it,' I told him. He left school with a respectable, if not outstanding, set of exam passes, but chose not to stay on into the sixth form, and I lost touch with him.

Staying Cool

A problem ...

Some years later, I had travelled by train to a neighbouring town and I was waiting outside the station to catch a taxi. Suddenly, a small car pulled up and a head leaned out of the window. 'Mr Lambillion! Wotcha! Where are you going?' It was the young man, now some years older, driving his own, very smart car. I remember thinking it was much smarter than the car I had left parked at home that morning!

He offered me a lift, which I gratefully accepted and on the journey I discovered that in partnership with a friend, he now owned two garages. He had worked hard and despite problems (challenges!) and setbacks, his vision and quiet determination had helped him achieve what he wanted to achieve. I was delighted for him. He told me it hadn't always been easy but he'd kept his focus, refused to give up and eventually got there.

Use Affirmations

Affirmations can help us achieve in our lives and can help us change conditions in ourselves and our circumstances, especially when accompanied by pictures and images which are consistent.

If you wish to try the use of affirmations:

1. Look at something in yourself you wish to improve. Perhaps you want to be calmer, to be happier, or simply to have a successful day.
2. Think of a way of writing that down as a simple statement.

    'Today I am positive and happy.'

    or

    'Today is a good day for me.'

    or

    'I am happy and calm at all times.'

... becomes a challenge.

Begin with yourself and your own issues and write your affirmation accordingly.

3. When you are happy with your affirmation, write it down in capital letters on a small piece of paper or card. You can perhaps write it in your journal or diary. Use bold, big letters. A positive statement needs positive letters. If you are artistic or enjoy decorating things, then you can colour it if you wish and maybe decorate around it. The important thing is that you can see the words clearly.
4. Next, take a pause, making a few of your deep breaths.
5. In your imagination, inside your head, build a simple picture to go with the idea. Make the picture as clear as you can and see yourself doing exactly what the affirmation says. During your day, keep the affirmation with you if at all possible and, in convenient private moments, you can have another look at it and say the words calmly inside your mind, seeing the same picture you constructed earlier. Keep the picture the same. Changing it confuses your mind and can slow things down.

This process will help you to feel different about yourself and your prospects, and if you persist, you will be surprised at what happens. Be patient, as it may take several days before changes will be seen, but you will develop an even greater sense of being in control of your life and what happens to you. I have used this approach with many young people, very successfully.

Affirmation for Others

When we have been working on your own issues for a while, it is important to look outwards and see how we

Happy and Positive

interact with others. One key idea is what we can loosely term 'seeing the good in others', and generally being optimistic. We can't expect others to be positive about us if we are not positive about them. Eventually we get what we give and so, for us to be happy and successful, it is important we give the same message to others.

Make an effort to see the good, the positive in others. Perhaps you can write a simple affirmation about others and your attitude to them.

'I see everyone as valuable.'

or

'I think everyone is important.'

or

'I can see good things in everyone I meet.'

Use the same process as earlier, writing the affirmation on a card and do as you did before, saying it three times and building a picture.

You can imagine a special glow about people, a lovely warmth, or perhaps picture a good 'heart to heart' connection between you and everyone else, as you did in the interview technique in Chapter 3.

Keep it simple and be persistent. Things may not happen straight away. They often don't but they will happen eventually. It will be worth every effort you make.

You may have a particular friend, relative or acquaintance who is having difficulty or experiencing a bad patch in his or her life. Of course, where you can, you should be supportive and caring when in the presence of that person and be encouraging and helpful.

But sometimes, it isn't necessary to say things or maybe not even possible to do so. Sometimes it is simply a question of 'being there' in the best way we can. And if we think good things about others, it alters our relationship to them and it is also sensed by them, even if we say nothing. To use a 1960s phrase, 'they pick up on our energy!' People also often say, 'Thanks for being there,' when we have supported them in some way in their lives. It is a wonderful thing to say and to have said about you too.

Having a constructive or good attitude about others will open doors for you, help others feel good about you and help you to feel good about yourself.

Be an affirmation for others; it's a great thing to be. If you find people being negative about themselves, encourage them, not in a pushy way, but gently and constantly and they will thank you for it in times to come.

And look for good things that are done for you and said to you by others. You may be surprised if you 'count your blessings' in this way. We live in a world where we are encouraged to think in the other direction, to see faults in others, to look for their weaknesses, which is so sad.

Our newspapers and media love gossip and are particularly guilty of this. But you don't have to be like this and your life will be all the better for it if you are not.

Nelson Mandela, someone who never gave up and who came to be leader of the country in which he was once imprisoned as a social outcast and political prisoner, made a wonderful speech that illustrates this negative conditioning and how we all hide behind it:

> Our deepest fear is not that we are inadequate.
> Our deepest fear is that we are powerful beyond measure.
> It is our light, not our darkness,

that most frightens us. We ask ourselves;
Who am I to be –
brilliant, gorgeous, talented, fabulous?

Actually, who are you not to be?
You are a child of God. Your playing
small doesn't serve the world.
There's nothing enlightened about
shrinking so that other people around
you won't feel insecure.

We are all meant to shine, as children do.
We are born to manifest the glory of God
that is within us.
It's not just in some of us; it's in
everyone. And as we let our light shine,
We unconsciously give other people permission
to do the same.

As we are liberated from our own fear,
Our presence automatically liberates others.

Affirming and thinking positively about yourself and about others will really let the light shine in you.

Setting Goals

Sometimes, it is possible to achieve things simply and quickly, especially our short-term goals. Other things may take longer, and are made of a series of steps or intermediate short-term goals. We learn skills, the short-term goals which are, in turn, the steps towards our bigger, longer-term goals, dreams or aspirations.

Staying Cool

If you are a musician, you have to practise your technique in stages, gradually playing more and more complicated pieces of music as your skill improves, until you can perform freely, playing whatever you wish to play. This is true of everything you do, in what we all do.

It is important to have goals and to work towards them in stages, patiently and carefully. You may have many goals. Some of them will be simple ones and some will be long-term ones.

1. Make two headings:
   - Goals and Dreams
   - 1: Long Term, 2: Short Term
2. Make a list of your short-term goals. They can be very simple, connected with an ambition to go somewhere, learn something, even earning and saving to buy something.
3. Next, number them in order of importance, e.g.
   - Finish chemistry homework.
   - Attend fitness class/gym regularly ... etc
   - Work a few extra shifts to save for a holiday.
   - Practise new chords on guitar.
4. Then do what you have to do to achieve each one.

Of course you cannot perhaps do this for everything, but it is useful to keep a list of short-term goals that you review on a regular basis, perhaps every few days and certainly once a week, and rewrite it. If any goal hangs around too long on the list, see what you can do to move it off to the next level or so.

This activity helps you to have some focused structure to the detail of your life. It helps you achieve what you both need to achieve and want to achieve. Sometimes they are the same thing, maybe sometimes not, but they all need to be done.

These little goals are the building blocks of your life. Many successful chemistry homeworks could lead to a science degree and a position in a good company as a researcher. Regular visits to the gym will keep you fit and help you to have the physical stamina for many things in your life over the years. You will know where your priorities are and how to select your goals.

Many people admire the marvellous football skills of David Beckham, especially those wonderful free kicks he takes with superb skill and accuracy for England and Manchester United. What few people realise is that he spends hours practising those skills. His manager, Sir Alex Ferguson, said that after other training has finished, David will practise those kicks alone on the training pitch for some time until he is happy with what he has achieved.

Likewise, Johnny Wilkinson, the amazing England rugby player: his wonderful kicks which have won England so many points in rugby internationals are practised for hours between games.

This practising is part of the short-term goal success. The achievement of lots of smaller goals helps us to achieve greater ones.

Another reason for listing short-term goals is that when we cross them off our list as they are achieved, we feel satisfaction, and maybe sometimes relief! We can see our progress in such a way.

Perhaps even more important, when we list what we need to achieve it takes the pressure off us. We do not have to carry it around in the front of our mind all the time like some hidden nagging worry. We can check our list and see how we are doing.

'Must Do: Want to Do!'

Of course, some goals, as I have said, are maybe 'must do's' and often, to achieve a bigger, longer-term objective, we may have to do some shorter, less attractive, less interesting 'must do's' on the way to bigger goal realisation.

But they are all important stepping stones on the way. Always say a little 'well done' to yourself and feel good when you achieve a 'must do' and a 'want to do'! Your mind will be impressed and want to achieve more.

Hopes and Dreams

Longer-term goals, often the dreams and hopes of what we want to achieve in life, are also important.

If we attend to the short-term 'must do's' and 'want to do's' then we are building towards those bigger pictures in our minds, those wonderful dreams and visions we have. Sometimes we don't achieve the goals we have exactly as they are, but we often get close to them. And they are important as they act like magnets, pulling us forward towards them.

My daughter is a fine musician. She had a goal to learn the violin, despite having tiny hands hardly suited to a string instrument. Over the years she worked through her short-term goals, the 'must do's' and the 'want to do's', in order to master her technique, pass the various exams (her short-term goals and stepping stones) to go to university and successfully study for a music degree.

Happy and Positive

Goal achieved, and she, like everyone does, experienced many problems, including a serious road accident which affected both her back and her vision. She had to overcome the difficulties of sitting for hours in one position whilst she played in the orchestra, at the same time having difficulty reading the music and seeing the conductor with her damaged vision.

However, she didn't wish to travel around as a professional musician, and so she taught for a while, also doing a little playing. This really wasn't her thing, but she remembered how she enjoyed, on her degree course, two optional modules of study she chose to do: 'Music and the Law', and 'Copyright'.

She had enjoyed them very much and unexpectedly was offered the chance to train as a lawyer and she is now doing this. Her goal of a music degree was important, and once achieved, it opened the door to something else. Now she has new goals to work towards: short-term law exams and practice and long-term, as a qualified lawyer.

So we have to be open to follow our goal and then, sometimes, as we reach it or get close to it, to open up to new goals, fresh dreams and hopes and see where they take us.

You may have a dream you wish to pursue which is clear and strong in your mind. So follow it. Have some long-term goals, some dreams and work towards them. Write them down and picture them in your imagination. If you can find a picture that symbolises them for you, in a magazine or newspaper, cut it out and stick it in your journal. Then work towards it through a series of short-term goals. Find out what you want to do, and do it. Never give up.

Energy and Talent

I heard a very famous author interviewed once on TV. It was on a programme about success and failure. The programme was considering what success is, and how many successful people have to overcome failures on their way to success, sometimes even having once been very successful, then have it all crash around them, to then build up again to more success.

He said that he had been successful in one area of life. Then it had all collapsed and fallen apart. Instead of sulking, he put his mind to things and started a new, very successful career as a writer. There are two things, he said, that are significant in our lives and in achieving our goals: Energy and Talent.

He said that of the two, energy was the most important. With energy, you keep going and ultimately you will succeed. Even people who seem to have a lot of talent, if they have no energy will often fail to achieve their goals in life. And he is correct. Talent is nothing without energy and effort.

But in my experience, everyone is talented. In the young people I see around me I am often amazed at what they can do, at how they think. Everyone is talented, so keep your energy directed towards your goals and you will achieve great and wonderful things. Remember the words from the film tune: 'When the going gets tough, the tough get going.'

Never give up.

Goals: a Meditation

This meditation exercise builds upon the earlier visualisation for success, taking you a little more deeply

Happy and Positive

into your awareness and creating a highly magnetic image that you will work towards, come what may, if you use the exercise regularly.

1. So, take a pause and take some rhythmic slow breaths as in your unstressing exercise.
2. As your breathing slows down, place in your old suitcase anything you wish to for the duration of this exercise.
3. Imagine a wave of beautiful calming energy washing through you, from your head downwards, until your entire body is relaxed and warmly comfortable.
4. Recall the energy points or centres that are aligned to your spine, and focus upon the point at the root of your spine. This is where your will power is based and imagine that symbolised as a clear, red light. Think the words 'I am calm and determined.'
5. Imagine that this red energy moves upwards into the space around your heart point, in the centre of your chest, where the light changes to green. Pause here for a moment and think the idea 'I am calm, determined and happy.'
6. Next, lift your focus upwards to the space behind the centre at your brow or forehead. As you do this, the colour changes to violet. Pause here and imagine clearly the goal you have at this time. See it in as much detail as you can, as if you are painting or drawing a picture. As you see the picture, smile and think, 'I am calm, determined, happy and will achieve my goals perfectly.'
7. Enjoy the picture for a while, before allowing it to fade.
8. And then, mentally climb down the steps you have climbed up. From violet, to green, to red.
9. Then focus on your breathing, allowing it to become rhythmic again.

10. Ground yourself by feeling the soles of your feet touching the ground. Open your eyes slowly and then go about your normal activities.

Alternatively ...

As an alternative, you can go through your rhythmic breathing as before, filling yourself with calm, cool energy, then:

1. Imagine you are standing at the door of a large, friendly house. Open the door. Your name is written on it in large letters.
2. Walk inside. In front of you are some stairs and to one side there is a small table with a message written on the top in large red letters. It says 'I am calm and determined.' Pause and read the words in your mind, before walking up the stairs to the next landing.
3. Here, there is another table with a message written on it in large green letters. It says 'I am calm, determined and happy.' Pause and read it to yourself before going up the stairs to the top of the house.
4. As you reach the top, open the door in front of you. It opens out into a comfortable room with a television and an armchair for you to sit on. Sit on the armchair and as you switch on the TV, a picture develops, first of all a circle of violet light and then it changes to a programme about you. In the picture you are achieving great things, happily reaching the creative goals you have set for yourself. In the film, you say, 'I am always calm, determined, happy and successful. I achieve my goals in life perfectly.'
5. Enjoy the programme, and then get up, leave the room and carefully go back down the stairs, pausing at the tables you saw on your way up.

6. Go out of the house and, again, look at your name above the door.
7. Finally, let the pictures fade, and return to your rhythmic breathing, grounding yourself and returning to normal consciousness slowly as you have done before.

If you wish, draw a diagram or picture of this last exercise, and use colour in it too. It will help to reinforce the idea in your mind and help to produce the magnetism necessary for you to attract success.

> Go confidently in the direction of your dreams. Live the life you've imagined!
> – Rousseau

Summary of Activities

- *The Smile Technique*

Focus on something that makes you happy and use the energy of the smile to unstress and calm your whole body, to make you feel good.

- *Use Affirmations*

Use positive, constructive statements and images throughout your day to change how you feel about yourself and others.

- *Setting Goals*

Practise setting yourself short-term and long-term goals and objectives. Work towards them, using your imagination to do so. Keep the vision!

- *Goals: A Meditation*

Meditate upon success and goals, using your energy centres, root (red), heart (green) and head (violet), to work up towards your goals and the powerful ideas in your imagination.

Chapter 6
Problems, Feelings and Making Things Work

So far, we have considered many simple, practical things that can help you to bring the best out of yourself; ways to help you become and remain cool and calm, to be focused and clear in your mind, and to work creatively towards your goals and dreams as you go through your life.

Practised regularly, these activities will help you to do all these things. You may still have problems or challenges from time to time, but your attitude towards them will be able to influence the outcome.

An angry, panicking attitude struggles and generally makes our problems appear greater than they are. A calm, constructive attitude will *always* find a way around difficult issues, towards solutions.

Remember:

- **A cool, calm, constructive attitude will find a way around all problems.**
- **A calm, constructive attitude finds solutions.**

Acceptance

Some years ago, a young man I knew aged 15, a very good sportsman, was suddenly and inexplicably picked on and bullied by his coach, someone he had respected, whom he had listened to and followed with great loyalty over a period of four years.

Neither he, nor anyone else, could understand this situation. The coach dropped him from the team, although he was still playing well, and was extremely unkind to him. No amount of effort to understand the coach's actions could get to the truth and the young lad was devastated.

However, after initial anger and frustration, the boy and his parents decided to let go of the situation and to accept that they could do nothing further about it. They had made their protests, but these had fallen on deaf ears in the official channels.

They decided that this situation was a bad and unhappy one. The boy had always loved his football and was a good player, but there was no point in fighting it. They accepted that things were as they were and that he was no longer at the football club, however unfair that seemed. But they also adopted the attitude that they could change things in the future, and that the boy could and would play football again, despite his confidence having been shattered.

A week of so later, they received a telephone call from a coach at a football club in a neighbouring town. This coach had heard that the player was available, and that he had been treated unfairly. He asked to sign him up at his club. It was a bigger club, with better facilities than the one the boy had left and he moved on and enjoyed the rest of the season there.

Problems, Feelings and Making Things Work

After a while, he could see that by being calm, accepting the reality of his situation, however aggrieved about it he was, he was able to attract to himself an opportunity to move on and ultimately improve things.

He learned an important rule. It is often called the principle of acceptance:

- **However bad things are, however unfair of difficult things seem, don't fight them. Stay cool. Accept the circumstances you are experiencing.**
- **But, and this is an important 'But', recognise that you can improve things, that things can and will improve.**
  - **Stay cool, calm and constructive.**
  - **Accept things as they are.**
  - **But then recognise you can change them and that circumstances will change for the better.**

You can even write yourself an affirmation on a card: *Things will now be getting better and better for me.*

This is a very important idea. Most of us are sometimes guilty of wasting energy, battling to change things back to how they were, or trying to deny the situation we find ourselves in: 'This isn't fair!' 'This can't be true,' 'I won't accept this,' and so on.

Calm and cool acceptance is the beginning of changing things for the better.

This doesn't mean we ignore injustice and don't try to put things right where we can, in a calm and constructive way and where applicable, by going down the correct channels to sort things out. But meeting conflict with conflict is always ineffective and denying something to be how it is, is also a self-defeating illusion. Once we accept that we can do no more, we free ourselves and our creative power to move on, into new situations. These will always come and help us leave behind our experience.

> **Calm acceptance creates the space for better things to come.**

Remember this, and use it in any difficult situation. You will find that the solutions will come to you more quickly and more easily if you do.

Journals and Diaries

I mentioned earlier in the book the value of keeping a diary or journal of some kind. It is useful, largely for two reasons.

First, it helps us to learn from our experiences. By noting down important things that happen to us, we can learn to see what new ideas come to us through them. We can learn to note down how we change and improve in the way we feel and the way we manage our lives.

We can also observe what situations keep repeating themselves, where similar things seem to happen, time and again. When they do, they are telling us something and telling us we have to change somehow.

Problems, Feelings and Making Things Work

By keeping notes on what we see as significant and important we can learn and gain insights, but perhaps most important, we are able to see how much we grow and develop as individuals. Look for that especially, for as the saying goes, 'Success breeds success.' Note down the small successes, the little breakthroughs, as well as the big ones, for great success is built upon many smaller successes, just as the achieving of greater goals is the consequence of achieving many smaller objectives on the way.

Noting such things down and recognising them impresses your subconscious and helps you to attract more success into your life by the manner in which you think and act.

A second reason for writing things down is that it helps you to release things, to let them go. By writing things down, your mind will automatically begin to file them away and help you to let go and move on. It is a form of unstressing and has a powerful effect. It helps you to draw a line under things and to let them go out of your mind and out of your life if necessary.

You may decide that there are some things you don't wish to keep in your journal. They may be temporary, passing events you simply wish to release. Those you can do on single sheets of paper and then, after reflecting on them for a day or so, throw them away.

Sometimes that is a useful way to let go of anger or frustration or to resolve an issue between yourself and another person.

Key Exercise: Clearing Unpleasant Feelings

Lizzie, a young friend of mine, had a problem with her sister. She found that whenever they were together they would argue, usually over the most trivial matters. She wanted to change this, yet found that as soon as they were together, the same old issues would come to the surface and war would break out once more between them. Lizzie began to ease the situation by writing things down, using the following steps.

If you are in such a situation, you try it.

1. Firstly, if someone or something is troubling you, write down how you feel about it all. Use whatever words you think are appropriate and really describe the feelings you have. When you have done that, take a few deep breaths, tear up your piece of paper and throw it away. It is not for anyone else to see. It was simply a way for you to release your tensions and some of your negative feelings. In addition, practise your unstressing exercises and also find someone you trust to talk to about it. Your parents and family or your school or college will help you with that. Releasing our feelings in a constructive way helps us to free ourselves from them and the harmful effects they may have upon us. You will certainly benefit by using such an approach.

2. Secondly, if you have a problem with a particular individual, then write him or her a letter; it is a letter you will never send. In this letter, you can say anything, so try to be constructive. Say how you wish things to be between you, how you know the situation can be better for both of you. Write some good things about the person, even if you find that difficult. There is something good in everyone, even if it seems to you that it is well hidden! Say how you realise in your heart that things can be okay, that you can both be happy in your lives, with no conflict.

Problems, Feelings and Making Things Work

Here is a sample letter to help you. You can change it and adapt it however you wish to. It is simply an example on which to base your letter.

Dear ___

I am sad because of the difficulties that I feel exist between us. However, I realise there are two sides to every story and it takes two to have a conflict. I also know, in my heart, that both you and I can enjoy our lives and be happy and fulfilled. I know there are good things in me and good things in you, and that we can get along okay. I'm sure things will improve between us now.
Sincerely

———

Then maybe decorate the letter with some bright patterns or colours if you wish. Be sure to write only constructive, positive ideas. This letter is confidential and for you only. It is not to be sent. But in writing it, you loosen up and begin to release the difficult feelings and energy between you both. When you have finished it, you can throw it away safely, where no one else will see or find it. Don't be ashamed or embarrassed by it. It will help you enormously. It is a very powerful thing for you to do.

My friend Lizzie, whom I mentioned earlier, wrote a version of this 'unsent' letter several times over many weeks. The next time she and her sister met, during the Christmas holidays, things were noticeably much easier and warmer. 'It was like magic,' said Lizzie. 'The tension between us had dissolved. It was so much better.'

Try this, in any difficult relationship. Of course, we have to take necessary action and advice where appropriate.

Saying Sorry!

And if necessary, and if you feel you are at fault, see if you can find a way to say sorry, to apologise, or to make things better.

Sometimes this can be difficult and we may feel a little embarrassed or awkward when doing it. But it is, again, a very powerful thing to do. People who can recognise their mistakes and recognise that they are possibly at fault in some way, and say sorry, are people who learn from their mistakes. They are strong people. And each time they apologise, they become stronger, more liberated people.

Where necessary, say sorry, and resolve to avoid conflict as much as possible. I studied and practised Martial Arts for some years and learned that true Martial Arts Masters, despite all their great combat and defence skills, would do everything they possibly could to avoid conflict. This is a good lesson to learn, and one that many western Martial Artists would do well to heed!

Others may apologise to you also, expressing their regret, and that is good and very healing. But if they don't, that's up to them. You are taking charge, taking the initiative and freeing yourself from unnecessary bad feelings and thoughts.

Try to be patient! It may take a few letters before you notice a difference, but it will come.

Releasing Anger

If you are angry with someone, it has the same effect upon you as being sad. Such feelings weaken you and may even

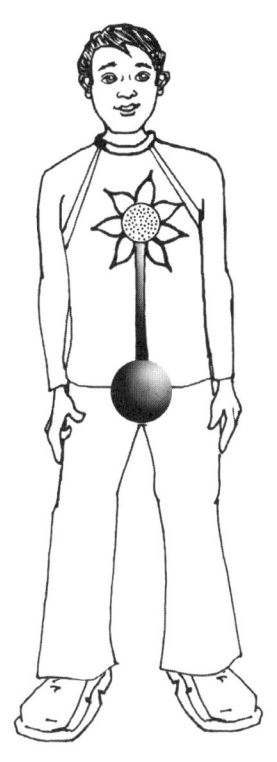

Releasing anger.

depress you if your anger stays with you for a long time.

It is important to deal with the source of your anger constructively if you can see how you can do that. But there is another way you can also free yourself from it.

1. Take a pause, close your eyes and develop your deep, rhythmic breathing as in the unstressing exercise.
2. Fill your body with calming energy and when you feel you have done that, focus on the energy point at the base of your spine.
3. Imagine there is a ball of red energy there. Place your 'angry' situation inside the ball, remembering who or what it is that has angered you.

4. Gradually imagine your red ball of energy rising slowly upwards along your spine. As it does so, it starts to change colour, changing from a strong fiery red, to a deep rose pink.
5. Let the rose colour rise up to the heart energy centre, which is level with the centre of your chest. As it reaches here, imagine the colour changing further into a beautiful, rose pink flower, surrounded by deep green leaves.
6. As you do this, your feelings of anger will dilute, becoming weaker and fainter.
7. Imagine picking off a few petals from your flower and gently tossing them into the breeze. As they fly away, think to yourself, 'I throw away my anger on the breeze.'
8. After a few moments, take some more of your deep, rhythmic breaths. You will feel calmer now and better.
9. Finally, ground yourself as you have done in earlier exercises before slowly opening your eyes and coming back to normal awareness.

You may need to do this a few times, but many people feel the benefit after one session.

My Boyfriend has Really Hurt Me!

One young girl I worked with was filled with anger over a cheating boyfriend. He had let her down badly. She had forgiven him, and he had done it again, this time with another girl. She was angry with both of them, but using this exercise she slowly began to feel better about the situation. She was able to let go of the anger she felt towards them and the depressing moments she had experienced as a consequence.

Slowly she became stronger and moved on in her life. It did not happen overnight. As she said to me, 'My boyfriend has really, really hurt me!' But by being angry, she was depleting her own energy, tiring and punishing herself further. She worked at it and it paid off for her.

Sometimes, we need to forgive more specifically, even when the anger has subsided.

Forgiveness

We often find forgiving a hard thing to do. When someone has really been awful to us, we may quite understandably find it difficult to let go. Our usual reaction is to want to retaliate, to get our own back, to make sure they 'pay' for whatever they have done to us or to someone we hold dear. We have often been conditioned in this way.

Karma

In the East, they have a philosophy of Karma. It is quite an intricate idea, but put in simple terms it means 'cause and effect', that what we do in life has an effect, not only upon others, but also on our circumstances and ultimately on ourselves. We have considered this indirectly earlier on.

Another expression to describe the same thing is, 'What goes around, comes around', or the biblical notion of reaping and sowing; in other words, what we get back in life is the result of what we do. Action brings Result.

No matter what your starting point in life, I can assure you this principle ultimately works through. My own children and I have spent many years discussing this idea and how it may work in our lives. There are obvious examples.

If you kick the door (cause/sowing) you may well damage it, and also hurt your foot (effect/reaping)! Obviously it is a daft thing to do, but it illustrates the basic principle in operation. I'm sure you can think of many others. I mention it in connection with forgiveness because the two things are related.

We can't expect ourselves to be forgiven for our own misdemeanours (after all, none of us is perfect) if we don't do the same for others. Equally, it is not our place to reek vengeance on others. Of course, if we break a civil or criminal law then our karma is to face the consequences in a court of law, plus the shame and embarrassment we may feel.

However, in our more personal issues, although we should always seek a just solution to every problem we may experience, or hurt and injustice that comes our way, we should remember the Law of Karma, that 'what goes around, comes around', and we should release ourselves from the hates or resentments which, like fear and anger, will only harm us in the long term.

As illustrated earlier on in the 'Mind over Matter' exercise, our thoughts affect the functioning of our physical bodies, and just as good, positive and constructive thoughts make us lighter and physically more efficient, so negative thoughts and feelings can weaken us over a long period of time, depressing our physical functions.

You don't need to carry around resentments. Using this little book offers you the opportunity to be 'Cool, Calm and Confident', fulfilled and successful.

Forgiveness gives you the chance to be free and I suggest to you here an exercise that I have used with old and young alike, in some form or another, with much success.

Forgiving Others

1. Take a pause, a few deep breaths and close your eyes for a moment, continuing to breathe deeply and rhythmically.
2. Now focus your attention in your head, where you see pictures in your inner screen, inside your mind.
3. Imagine yourself to be the pilot of a wonderful aeroplane, a little two-seater plane, flying through the air. Smile! You are happy and calm and enjoying yourself.
4. Below you in the field, you see the figure of someone you know, someone for whom you have held a resentment or severe dislike.
5. This is your chance to let go of that resentment, that dislike. In the seat behind you, is a large ball of snow, soft, fluffy white snow. Lift the ball of snow and drop it until it falls on the person below, shattering safely into white dust as it touches him or her. The person smiles and waves to you, having enjoyed the fun.
6. Circle your plane and wave goodbye as the person walks away, waving to you. You land your plane safely.
7. Then slowly return to normal consciousness, grounding yourself through your feet, before opening your eyes.
8. Later on, repeat the experience, only this time, you are on the ground and the other person flies the plane, dropping soft, fluffy white snow on you, harmlessly. This is important. However hard done by you may feel, there is always a two-way element to any dispute, any situation which results in bad feeling.

And if you don't like snow, you can use soft jelly, trifle, or ice cream instead. The effect will be the same. You may have to do the imagining for this a few times, but it will work if you give it a try!

Forgiving Yourself

Sometimes, we are angry with ourselves. In fact, most of our frustration can ultimately be traced back to how we become frustrated with ourselves.

We feel we have failed sometimes, let ourselves down or let others down. We forget that our failures are really opportunities, opportunities to learn, to regroup and to try again.

Remember that you often learn far more from your failures than you do from success. Of course, success is important and we should all feel good and savour those wonderful moments when our hard work and effort bear fruit. And we should remember those successes. They keep us going in the more difficult times. But in our difficulties we often discover strengths we didn't know we had. We can be amazed at our resourcefulness.

A young man of 17 years I did some work with was most distraught when I first met him. His mother had died and he was full of sadness and guilt. Sadness, because obviously he missed his mother very much and guilt because he remembered the times he'd argued with her or been uncooperative with her. He also felt powerless, as she lay sick with her terminal liver cancer. He felt he had let her down. Despite some bereavement counselling, his aunt brought him to see me. Over a few sessions, we discussed many things and did a few meditations and exercises.

Although she was no longer physically alive, he wrote a letter to his mother. He told her how much he loved her; how he regretted not doing the things he wished he had done, but never gotten around to. He also said sorry to her for when he was deceitful, uncooperative and had made life difficult for her. This was one of those valuable unsent letters, which spoke volumes and helped release tensions from him.

The experience also strengthened him for the future. He resolved to move on in life, with a stronger, more caring heart, deciding to train as a social worker with the disabled when he had finished his education.

He also did the following exercise, which he found useful.

1. First, take a pause and go into your calm space as you did at the beginning of Chapter 4.
2. As before, go inside your garden, or along your beach until you find a small pond or pool of water. This water is clear and still, reflecting only the clear light of a blue sky or the silver light of the moon.
3. Sit by this pond or pool of water for a moment. Notice how clear and smooth the surface of the water is. Drop a little pebble into the centre of the pool. Watch the splash and the ripples as they flow to the edge of the pool, gradually fading as they do so, until again the water is clear and still once more. Repeat this again, twice, each time seeing the pool clear until it is smooth, like a mirror.
4. Then see your own face reflected in the water, and as you see it, you smile. Your face is quite beautiful. You are a special person, unique and gifted, and you are needed by life. Life needs you to do wonderful things, and that you will do.
5. Gently drop another pebble into the pool and as the ripples clear across the reflection of your face, let them

take away with them the guilt and any sad feelings you may still have. Let them wash everything away. You're an okay person, doing the best you know how. You are learning as you go and growing into a stronger person.
6. Enjoy your calm space again for a few moments before leaving. Focus on your breathing, establishing a deep rhythm by saying the words 'I breathe in,' pause, 'I breathe out.'
7. Ground yourself through your feet, feeling the floor beneath you. Slowly open your eyes and return to normal awareness. In this moment, maybe write down a little affirmation, such as 'I forgive myself. I now move on to greater things.' Or 'I move on now.' Think it or say it to yourself three times, and then let it go.

And do a small, unrequested, nice thing or good turn for someone. Something simple and kind. This will reinforce the release of negative feelings, and also it is a lovely, empowering thing to do.

This exercise helped the young man considerably. It may well help you at some time.

Feeling Awkward and Shy

We all have moments when we feel awkward, maybe a little shy, especially as we grow, cease to be children, and learn to be adults. Many of us also feel awkward with the opposite sex as we grow up and realise we don't have much, if any, experience of these things. Experience is our greatest teacher. It's the way we all learn how to grow and develop our social skills, our ways and means of interacting with others.

The important thing to remember is our uniqueness. People are like snowflakes, all very similar in general appearance but beautifully special and different in detail. That is true of you, and life needs you; otherwise you wouldn't be here in the first place. The calmness you are learning will help you to dilute and reduce any shyness or uncomfortable feelings you may have from time to time.

An important attitude to develop is that of realising that everyone you meet is important. Even those you don't like. They are important. And so are you.

- You are unique.
- You are important.
- You have a specialness that no one else has.

Think 'snowflake' and remember we are all similar but different. And that includes you. The following exercise will help you.

Feeling Good About Yourself

1. Stand upright, with your feet slightly apart.
2. Imagine a glow of golden light in your solar plexus, like bright sunlight.
3. Allow this light to really grow and radiate, pouring down your body, through your legs and feet and into the earth.
4. Imagine you have roots, like a wonderful tree. Like the tree, you are strong, powerful and magnificent.
5. Think of yourself then radiating wonderful light all around you, like a bright sun. Let yourself feel really sunny.

This radiance will touch other people. They will notice you and see you in a wonderful, positive light. It will make you more magnetic, so you attract good things into your life.

When you have done this, sit down for a moment and write down five good things about yourself, anything positive you can call to mind that you could tell others about you and your gifts. They can be big things or small things. It doesn't matter. Just write them down and read them through a few times. If you do this from time to time, it will help you to radiate and really shine, wherever you are and whatever you are doing.

Laughing It Off

I knew a young man who was rather accident prone and often seemed to get himself into embarrassing situations, situations which provoked others to laugh at him. He developed a great technique for dealing with mishaps and some awkward situations: he laughed them off! If he dropped something, he didn't react by being embarrassed, trying to cover it up as if it hadn't happened, or maybe even getting angry. Instead, he would laugh. He would make a light joke of things so that he laughed with people, rather than them laughing at him.

Try to do this sometimes. If something appears to go wrong or you have a mishap, try to see the funny side of it. See it in your mind like a funny cartoon. Doing this will change how you feel about the situation and how others feel about it also, in a very positive way.

If you feel a little awkward or shy, smile; the smile will also help you glow and help you feel good. Practise it and practise laughing off the silly little hiccups that happen to you!

Problems, Feelings and Making Things Work

Exercise and Diet

To make the most of yourself, it is important to mention a few simple tips in relation to exercise and diet here.

Do take some regular exercise. Such things are vital if you wish to have a healthy, happy life. In this age of the car and the television remote control, we in the West, in particular, tend to take far less exercise than the generations before us, and consequently, we are physically less healthy. Diseases associated with lack of exercise are on the increase, and obesity is becoming a real problem in young and old alike.

Many of you may ride bicycles, or dance, or participate in some regular activity of some kind. But some of you may not.

Good supervised activities such as yoga, martial arts, tai chi, swimming and most sports are ideal. They tone and exercise your body and create a good physical home in which your mind and its abilities can flourish.

If you enjoy dancing, do it often. But one of the best forms of exercise is walking. It puts little unnecessary stress on joints and limbs, and is easy to do. Most of us can walk. So try to walk often.

Take a walk that is at least a couple of miles long several times a week. As you walk, quicken your pace for a while, to exercise your heart and lungs, putting more oxygen into your blood and your body, and your brain!

Make a point of walking when it is possible to do so. You will feel so much better for it. As young children, we usually wanted to walk, whilst our parents wanted us to get back into the pushchair as they were in a hurry and our slower pace slowed them down! But make walking a daily activity, sometimes walking for longer than usual.

Eat well and eat good food. Our food has become increasingly chemicalised and low on nutrients, processed to ridiculous lengths, so there is little or no goodness left in it.

If you are in doubt about your diet, do consult a dietician, or if you are still at school, talk to a teacher qualified in that area who will, I am sure, be only too pleased to help you.

Remember to include fresh fruit and vegetables in your diet on a daily basis. 'An apple a day keeps the doctor away' is an old saying based upon good principles. And restrict convenient junk food to the odd occasion rather than having it as a regular feature of your eating pattern.

Good fresh fruits and vegetables and good, organically reared proteins, will keep your body healthy. They will give your mind every chance to excel and for you to do everything in life you wish to do. Try to avoid the chemicalised rubbish that dominates so many of our supermarket shelves.

Creativity: Music, Art and Recreation

A busy study and examination schedule often means we stop doing the things we loved to do when we were younger. Those creative things that are so vital in our development as individuals, playing that guitar, violin or singing, painting, drawing, model making, writing poetry or stories, acting in plays and performances. These are important for us, and may even be part of our normal school or college curriculum.

For yourself, see if you can build into your schedule some creative recreation, preferably things that are not particularly linked to what you *have* to do for your studies.

Problems, Feelings and Making Things Work

It doesn't matter what it is, so long as it is open, and not dictated by any other need like an exam syllabus or test. Do something free, for enjoyment, something that uses your imagination and has no creative boundaries.

1. The exercises in this book will stimulate and strengthen your imagination. Use that impetus to write a poem or play that guitar that has been standing around for a while, gathering dust. Do a drawing or simple colouring activity.
2. Try 'doodling'. Have a few coloured pens or pencils and, whilst relaxing, just make a pattern as the mood takes you – shapes, symbols – whatever comes. We have all done this at times, on a pad whilst we talk on the phone, or on an old envelope whilst we are thinking through an idea or problem. Whatever it is, put in some doodling sometime and enjoy! You may be surprised at what happens.
3. If you like poetry, read it. I do, most days, and it is part of my 'unstressing' programme.
4. Listen to a variety of music, and go to concerts. Visit art galleries and exhibitions. In such a way you put yourself in touch with good, creative influences and may stimulate yourself to be creative also. A creative mind is a healthy mind, so have some creative fun from time to time.
5. And remember the other balance –
Work, Rest and Play.

    We need to work, to test and develop ourselves. We need also to rest, to take time out from all activity so we can sleep and cool down mentally and physically.

    And we need a little play. Have some fun from time to time.

Ensure you have good sleep, including some early nights. Most youngsters, and I was exactly the same, see sleep as a nuisance. Remember to have good, regular sleep.

You can still find time for fun!

Summary of Activities

- *Key Exercise: Clearing Unpleasant Feelings*
   (a) Write down your feelings, then throw the paper away.
   (b) Write, in a constructive way, the letter that is never sent.

- *Saying 'Sorry'*

It is a powerful thing to do when you *know* you are in the wrong.

- *Releasing Anger*

Learn to release anger by using the colour change technique, lifting the feeling up from the energy centre at the root of your spine through your heart, as it turns into a beautiful flower.

- *Forgiving Others*

Forgive others using your magic aeroplane and snowball or trifle.

- *Forgiving Yourself*

Forgive yourself and let go of guilty feelings by visiting your calm inner space, looking into your pool of water and using the ripples your pebble makes as it briefly disturbs the surface, to wash them away.

- *Feeling Good about Yourself*

This is a simple exercise to develop inner radiance.

- *Creativity: Music, Art and Recreation*

Practise creative ways of relaxing and resting.

Chapter 7
And so ... Getting Physical!

As well as calming the mind, we also need to be attentive to our physical selves and do things which can help to loosen us up in simple ways. There are many mental activities and techniques already presented in these pages, some of which will seem more useful to you than others, more relevant to you and your situation.

The Key Exercises and particularly the Unstressing ones, in my experience, will be useful to everyone if practised regularly.

Practice is important. Practise when you feel okay. Try not to wait until you are under pressure to learn basic unstressing and relaxation techniques. It is easier to develop the techniques *before* you may think you need them. Then the tensions won't be so difficult to deal with and you may well find the excesses of stress may simply not build up in you in the first place if you have been working at your technique for even just a few days or weeks.

One young student I worked with on unstressing techniques faced a challenge within a fortnight of coming to see me, when she discovered her beloved dog was ill and

And so ... Getting Physical

needed urgent treatment. 'I was much calmer than usual,' she told me with more than a little surprise when she heard the news. Be patient and committed and it will surely pay off.

My experience also suggests that most people, in the early days, find it easier to work with a recording of the exercise. One group of students I am currently working with found this to be the case, so I prepared a recording of the basic exercises for them that they were then able to use to make individual copies.

Again, I suggest you do this for yourself, or if you wish to, use someone else's voice. Ask a friend, parent or teacher to do it for you. If you are working in a group, which is a good idea once in a while, then you can do the recordings between you if necessary. Also, on page 176 is an email address, and you can contact my office for any further help relating to the commercially available cassettes I have which may help you.

You may also find some very simple stretching exercises useful to do. We have done much which will help calm your mind, enhance your creativity and increase your confidence.

Here are a few more simple techniques to try for your mind *and* body.

For the Beginning of the Day

(a)
- Place your hands either side of your head, with your finger tips lightly touching your scalp.
- Gently rotate your fingers all together, massaging the skin and tissue around the skull. Do this for a minute or

so and it will increase the circulation, helping to clear your head after sleep.
- You can do this before an examination or test.

(b)
- Loosen your neck as described earlier in the book, by doing some gentle neck rotations.
- Pay particular attention to letting your head rest gently on each shoulder for a few seconds, before carefully moving your head back to the upright position and then onto the other shoulder.

(c)
- Stand upright, with your feet slightly apart.
- Place your hands on your hips and rotate your hips in a circle three times in a clockwise direction and three times anti-clockwise. This will loosen your lower back and your spine and legs generally.

(d)
- Rotate your left shoulder by placing your left hand on your chest, with your elbow pointing out sideways.
- Then, rotate your elbow in a big circle three times in each direction – forwards then backwards. Imagine there is a piece of chalk on the tip of your elbow that is drawing the circle.
- Then repeat for your right shoulder.

Eye Relaxation

If you are going to do a lot of reading, writing, or computer work, the following exercises are very useful.

And so ... Getting Physical!

(a)
- Place a fingertip at the end of your eyebrow, near the top of your nose.
- Applying very gentle pressure, move your finger along your eyebrow, then down around the eye socket, across the top of the cheekbone and back up to the point you started at.
- Keep your finger pressing gently at that point, before repeating the movement twice more.
- Repeat this with both eyes, massaging with gentle pressure as you move your finger around your eye socket.

(b)
- Place your right index finger gently against your right temple on the side of your head. It is the slight dip, just behind your eyes.
- Applying very slight pressure, rotate your finger five times in a forward direction, and then five times backwards, making small circles as you do so.
- Repeat the exercise with your left hand and left temple.

(c)
- With your head upright, look straight ahead.
- Slowly move your eyes upwards to the right, to look as far as you can comfortably do so, into the right-hand corner of your vision.
- Keep your head facing forwards and slowly count to five.
- Then slowly move your eyes downwards to the opposite corner of your vision, looking to the bottom left-hand corner.

- Again, keep you head facing forwards and count slowly to five.
- Repeat this exercise, this time moving your eyes to the top left of your vision and then down to the bottom right, holding each position for a count of five.

All these exercises increase the flow of blood and energy around your eyes. If your eyes have been especially heavily used and strained, you can also do the following:

- Pour some water into two small bowls, one warm (not hot!) and one cold (not freezing!).
- Close your eyes and bathe the eyelids and surrounding skin gently with the warm water for a few moments. You can use a flannel or some cotton wool to do this.
- Gently dry your eyes on a soft towel and then repeat the exercise using the cold water.
- You can do this two or three times. It will soothe and freshen your eyes naturally and safely.

The eye exercises are also useful before an examination or test of any kind.

Feeling Sluggish?

If you are feeling sluggish, or not properly awake or alert, the following is very simple and useful. It will also help to link the activity of both hemispheres of your brain and may be useful before an exam. I realise you may not wish to do this in front of others, but you can do it quickly and quietly, elsewhere, or before you leave home.

- Stand upright.

And so ... Getting Physical!

- Lift your left knee upwards and as you do so, touch it with your right hand.
- Repeat, this time lifting your right knee to your left hand.
- Do this slowly to start with, and then repeat it several times, perhaps a little more quickly.

You can also do this lying down, on your back, lifting alternate knees to touch them with the opposite hand.

At the End of the Day

- Lie with your back on the floor, knees bent upwards, feet about eighteen inches apart and arms outstretched to your side.
- Slowly lower your knees to the left, as far as you can, keeping your back on the floor, and turning your head to the right as you do so.
- Stay in that position for a count of five and return to your starting position.
- Repeat, by lowering your knees to your right, as far as you can go, keeping your back flat on the floor, this time turning your head to the left. Again, stay in that position for a count of five before returning to your starting position.

Repeat the whole exercise at least five times. It will help to release any accumulated tensions from your body and increase your energy flow.

Once you have mastered the exercise you can develop it and make it even more effective as follows:

- Before beginning the exercise, take a deep breath into your solar plexus.

- As you lower your knees towards the floor and move your head, slowly exhale, releasing your breath from your body.
- Breathe in again as you return to the starting position, with your knees bent pointing to the ceiling.
- Again, exhale as you lower your knees to the other side before returning to the upright position.

Massage Your Feet!

There are now many natural therapies that are either based on the massaging of the feet, or incorporate it in some way – reflexology, zone therapy, metamorphic technique and so on. They are very effective and very unstressing. There is a technique based on a Japanese tradition called *Do-in*, a self-massaging approach.

You can perform a simple technique for yourself as follows. This is especially good at the end of the day.

- Using your thumb and fingertips, massage gently across the base of each foot for a few minutes. Start with your right foot and then do the left. If you have time, you can use either a little talcum powder or massage oil; peppermint oil is especially good.
- Next, using only your thumb, massage the tips of each toe, working across your foot from big toe to the smallest one. Gently rotate your thumb as you massage them. Do the same for both feet.
- Then, again using your thumb, massage from the top of your big toe moving slowly along the inside edge of the toe, and along the inside edge of your foot until you reach your heel. Do this on both feet.
- Finish by massaging the entire base of each foot with

your thumbs and fingers once again, gently and carefully.

And a Little Help from Colours

You can probably think of colours and the associations and meanings they have for you. My daughter, now aged 26, always liked pink when she was small. Today, even as an adult, she still likes various shades of rose pink, and often buys clothes and household items with some pink in them.

There is a complete school of theory based on colour and its effects, the way in which colours affect our moods and feelings.

An experiment in a police station some years ago involved painting one of the cells pink. They found that when aggressive, sometimes drunken individuals were placed inside, the rose pink had a profound calming effect upon them. The police were really surprised.

Colour therapy is a significant art and there are a few colours you can use to help you in particular situations. I use colour a lot in my own practice and the work I do with individuals.

Concentration
- Before tests, exams or any stressful situation or period of deep concentration, close your eyes for a moment and imagine the colour yellow – beautiful, clear primrose yellow.
- Imagine the colour as a small ball of bright light inside your head.

- Let the colour grow and grow inside until it fills your head.
- Think the words 'I think clearly. I concentrate perfectly.' Then slowly open your eyes.

To assist your visualisation, find a yellow pencil and colour a large ball of yellow on a piece of paper, before you place the colour inside your head. Do this with each colour if you find it helps you.

Cooling Down

A quick way to cool down is to use the colour blue.
- Imagine a clear, sky blue light above your head.
- Allow that colour to flow through your head, your neck, your chest and arms, your stomach, legs and feet.
- See your entire body full of vibrant sky blue.
- Say in your head 'I feel cool and calm.'

Changing Times

If you are going through a period of change, perhaps starting a new school or college year, a new job, or leaving something behind, use the colour emerald green.
- Imagine the colour green in the centre of your body, near to the heart energy centre.
- Let this bright emerald green grow in size until it fills the centre of your body.
- Think the words 'I am looking forward to new things, to new people, new opportunities.' 'I am happy to change, to grow.'

Feeling Flat or Low on Energy

Orange light can give you more power and more energy when you feel tired, listless or simply worn out.

- Visualise a small ball of orange energy in your solar plexus.
- Imagine that ball of orange light growing and growing in size until it becomes almost golden in colour, filling your whole physical body from head to toe.
- Say to yourself, 'I am filling with power.' 'I am full of energy.'

Sleep

Rose pink helps with calming and especially for sleep. In fact, the rose and blue both have calming qualities and you can try either for this exercise:

- Imagine you are holding a beautiful deep pink rose.
- Let the colour from that rose flow into your head, just like a beautiful rose perfume. As it fills your head, say the words, 'I am calm and relaxed.' 'I will now sleep deeply and perfectly.'

And so you will!

Conclusion

This book will give you good strategies for *staying cool* and being more in control of your life.

Perhaps it is useful here to again consider some of the key ideas.

Remember to *take a pause* every day, a moment when you stop, take space, and quieten everything down in your mind and body. This is vital and will immediately be beneficial to you. (Chapter 1)

When you feel your mind is cluttered, as you probably will do from time to time, with lots of thoughts and ideas, and when you wish to be still and quieten your mind remember your *mental suitcase*. Maybe draw a picture of it or make it even more effective (remember your mind is very impressed by images) and put unwanted and irrelevant thoughts into it, shutting the lid down.

Resolve to develop and practise the *unstressing yourself* exercises (Chapter 2) with slow, deep and rhythmic breathing. This is such a valuable technique and along with developing a deeper long-term calmness, and mental

Conclusion

clarity, it is a technique that can 'rescue you' in difficult situations and quickly calm you down and help you to *stay cool*.

If you are having a problem sleeping or getting off to sleep, practise your *duvet technique*, deep, slow breathing that will rock you off to sleep as your duvet rises and falls like the sea! (Chapter 2)

To help your *creativity and improve your memory*, link the two hemispheres of your brain, so you benefit from the power of 'Whole Brain' learning. You can find some pleasant Vivaldi, such as the famous 'Four Seasons' or the 'Guitar Concerto' or Bach's 'Brandenburg Concertos' to help you with this. The rhythm and structure of such music is especially helpful for this purpose.

In *interviews and exams*, stay cool. Read questions three times, linking with them through your heart to really connect with them so your mind can clearly interpret what they are asking of you and then search into your *mental filing cabinet* for the information. You have put it there, so you can find it as you need it. It is always there.

In a *live interview*, connect your heart to those of the interviewers. They will then truly understand who you are and the interview will have the right outcome.

After a while, use your 'pause' time to create a *calm space*. You will develop a marvellous resource if you do this, that you can visit as you wish. This will also stimulate your imagination, so that you can use it to create a successful future for yourself, whatever it is that you do. (Chapter 4)

Sadness comes to us all sometimes. Seek help with issues that make you feel sad, and familiarise yourself with the *three steps method* (Chapter 4) to release those feelings that weigh you down, including the *fingers and thumbs* technique for recalling a happy, positive idea to replace negative ones.

Use *affirmations* – positive, constructive statements that help to change how you think and feel about yourself and others. And practise smiling. Even when we pretend to smile, the brain still releases the endorphins, the brain chemicals that make us feel good inside ourselves. Be a *smiler*.

Most of us get *angry* and *develop unpleasant, uncomfortable feelings*. Remember that you can *release anger and frustration* (Chapter 6) in a managed and constructive way, and also let go of *unpleasant feelings*.

And be creative!

For most of the exercises in the book, it is good to do a sketch or cartoons to go with it, just for the fun of it. You don't have to be an artist. It also helps to reinforce the idea in your mind.

But be creative in your life, and do something, music, art, writing, dancing or whatever you choose, to encourage creative, positive energies to flow through you and your mind. Creative people tend to be attractive, successful and interesting people.

Have some physical activity in your life. It doesn't have to be excessive, although the gym works for many, and such things as yoga, tai chi, karate and so on are good, structured ways to be *cool* and *physical*.

And finally, remember you are a *unique, wonderful and powerful* individual. Always remember this. Have that image in your mind: *attractive, radiant and special*. It is the truth about you. As you grow to understand this about yourself, you will not only help yourself, but also help

Conclusion

others to get in touch with their own gifts and talents, and make their way through life, *staying cool.*

Paul Lambillion's email address is:

paullambillion@dial.pipex.com

Staying Cool

How to Heal and Be Healed
A Guide to Health in Times of Change

Paul Lambillion

We live in a time of emotional and mental overload, which is approaching crisis proportions. There is a rapid growth in mental and emotional illnesses and a consequent explosion in the use of psychoactive drugs. There are the new energy diseases such as post-viral syndrome, ME, fatigue, exhaustion, intermittent depression and so on. These have no pathological framework to explain them, and there is usually no specific treatment structure for them. They affect young and old.

Using his long and successful experience of working with subtle energies, Paul Lambillion shows how these and other conditions can be addressed. Explaining the powerful effects of emotions and feelings on physical health, he provides a clear and persuasive framework for healing.

Throughout the book there are numerous exercises based on such techniques as breathing and visualisation, the use of energy essences, creativity and meditation. There are also many case histories.

This is a perfect healing manual that is wise, balanced and practical for our fast-changing times.

ISBN 0 7171 3415 6

From all good bookshops or directly from
www.gillmacmillan.ie

Auras and Colours
A Guide to Working with Subtle Energies

Paul Lambillion

Some people are gifted with the ability to see auras, the coloured energy sheath we all have around our physical bodies. An aura reveals an individual's spiritual, mental, emotional and physical state; their personality, gifts, aptitudes and other personal characteristics. Even inanimate objects have auras, as do animals, flowers, trees, houses, communities and cities.

Paul Lambillion teaches people how to discern auras and use this gift in a constructive way so that they can become more effective people and better healers. In this unique book, *Auras and Colours,* he presents a course in learning to understand our subtle bodies, which can bring a deep perception of the whole human being. It includes many useful exercises and meditations, helping us to unfold our own vision of colours and auras.

In addition, the author gives much information on the meanings of the colours and how an understanding of them can bring harmony to our everyday lives.

'With clear illustrations, useful exercises and easy writing style, Paul Lambillion presents a course in learning to understand our energy bodies, which can bring harmony to our everyday lives.'

Psychic News

ISBN 0 7171 3232 3

From all good bookshops or directly from
www.gillmacmillan.ie